Elizabethan England

Elizabeth I and Her Court

Other titles in The Lucent Library of Historical Eras, Elizabethan England, include:

Great Elizabethan Playwrights
A History of the Elizabethan Theater
Life in Elizabethan London
Primary Sources

The Lucent Library of Historical Eras

Elizabethan England
Elizabeth I and Her Court

William W. Lace

LUCENT BOOKS®

THOMSON

GALE

San Diego • Detroit • New York • San Francisco • Cleveland • New Haven, Conn. • Waterville, Maine • London • Munich

THOMSON
★
GALE

On Cover: Artist Robert Peake depicts Queen Elizabeth being carried in procession.

LIBRARY OF CONGRESS CATALOGING-IN-PUBLICATION DATA

Lace, William W.
    Elizabeth I and her court / by William W. Lace
        p. cm. — (The Lucent library of historical eras: Elizabethan England)
    Summary: A biography of England's Queen Elizabeth I, looking as well at the mem-
bers of her court and how they served her.
    Includes bibliographical references and index.
    ISBN 1-59018-098-4 (hardback : alk. paper)
    1. Elizabeth I, Queen of England, 1533–1603—Juvenile literature. 2. Great Britain—
History—Elizabeth, 1558–1603—Juvenile literature. 3. Great Britain—Court and
courtiers—History—16th century—Juvenile literature. 4. Queens—Great Britain—
Biography—Juvenile literature. [1. Elizabeth I, Queen of England, 1533–1603. 2. Great
Britain—History—Elizabeth, 1558–1603. 3. Great Britain—Court and courtiers. 4. Kings,
queens, rulers, etc. 5. Women—Biography.] I. Title. II. Series: the Lucent library of historical eras: Elizabethan England.
    DA355. L325 2003
    942.05′5′092—dc21
    [B]

                                                                                          2002008119

Printed in the United States of America

Contents

Foreword

Looking back from the vantage point of the present, history can be viewed as a myriad of intertwining roads paved by human events. Some paths stand out—broad highways whose mileposts, even from a distance of centuries, are clear. The events that propelled the rise to power of Germany's Third Reich, its role in World War II, and its eventual demise, for example, are well defined and documented.

Other roads are less distinct, their route sometimes hidden from view. Modern legislatures may have developed from old tribal councils, for example, but the links between them are indistinct in places, open to discussion and interpretation.

The architecture of civilization—law, religion, art, science, and government—as well as the more everyday aspects of our culture—what we eat, what we wear—all developed along the historical roads and byways. In that progression can be traced every facet of modern life.

A broad look back along these roads reveals that many paths—though of vastly different character—seem to converge at a few critical junctions. These intersections are those great historical eras that echo over the long, steady course of human history, extending beyond the past and into the present.

These epic periods of time are the focus of Lucent's Library of Historical Eras. They shine through the mists of history like beacons, illuminated by a burst of creativity that propels events forward—so bright that we, from thousands of years away, can clearly see the chain of events leading to the present.

Each Lucent Library of Historical Eras consists of a set of books that highlight various aspects of these major eras. For example, the Elizabethan England library features volumes on Queen Elizabeth I and her court, Elizabethan theater, the great playwrights, and everyday life in Elizabethan London.

The mini-library approach allows for the division of each era into its most significant and most interesting parts and the exploration of those parts in depth. Also, social and cultural trends as well as illustrative documents and eyewitness accounts can be prominently featured in individual volumes.

Lucent's Library of Historical Eras presents a wealth of information to young readers. The lively narrative, fully documented primary and secondary source quotations, maps, photographs, sidebars, and annotated bibliographies serve as launching points for class discussion and further research.

In studying the great historical eras, students also develop a better understanding of our own times. What we learn from the past and how we apply it in the present may shape the future and may determine whether our era will be a guiding light to those traveling future roads.

Introduction:
The One Sun

On a chilly November morning in 1558, a young woman stood reading under an oak tree at the pleasant English country house of Hatfield. Though her eyes were on the book, Elizabeth Tudor's thoughts very likely lay miles to the south in London. There, she knew, her half sister, Queen Mary I, lay gravely ill.

Suddenly, riders appeared, heading toward her at full gallop. They flung themselves out of their saddles and knelt at her feet. Elizabeth knew immediately why they had come. Mary was dead. Elizabeth had survived twenty-five years of plots, intrigue, scandal, disgrace, and imprisonment to become queen of England. She knelt on the dewy grass, clasped her hands together, and quoted, in Latin, a verse from the Book of Psalms: "This is the Lord's doing, and it is marvelous in our eyes."[1]

The reign of Queen Elizabeth I would, indeed, be marvelous—in the eyes of her subjects, the eyes of the rest of Europe, and the eyes of people in centuries to come. She inherited a country torn by

Princess Elizabeth would become queen of England at age twenty-five.

religious strife, impoverished by foreign entanglements. She would leave a strong, vigorous nation destined to become a great empire. The gloom of Mary's reign would give way to the brilliant splendor of Elizabeth's court.

The royal court was like the solar system. Like some planets, a few members of the court loomed large; others, smaller. Some had satellites of their own. Everything, however, revolved around one sun—the queen. Members of the court shined, but only in reflection of her light. There was no question who was the focal point, and those who forgot that fact were swiftly reminded. Once, when the countess of Leicester came to court dressed as extravagantly as Elizabeth herself, the queen boxed her ears, declaring "that as there was one sun that lighted the earth, so there should be one at Court."[2]

The *Curia Regis*

The royal court had been a fixture in England for five hundred years. It was introduced by William the Conqueror, the French duke who successfully invaded the island in 1066, defeating the Anglo-Saxon inhabitants. William surrounded himself with a handful of loyal noblemen to help him rule what was still a largely hostile land. This group was known as the *curia regis,* Latin for king's court.

At first, the members of the court dealt exclusively with military and administrative matters. They also helped the king administer justice, and this function eventually split off to become courts of

law. As the gulf in status between king and nobles increased, the court grew larger and began to take on household duties as well. For example, the chamberlain supervised the king's personal quarters. The chancellor attended to his spiritual needs. The steward saw that the entire household was properly run. Members of the nobility were honored to hold such titles, although others did the actual day-to-day work.

Still, the English royal court throughout the Middle Ages—roughly A.D. 1100 to 1500—was far from the elegant center of culture it would become under Elizabeth. Little attention was paid to learning or the arts, and even nobles might be illiterate. Castles were built for strength against invasion instead of comfort for those within. Members of the ruling class cared much more about fighting than about fashion.

European courts began to move toward elegance and refinement in Italy after the rebirth of culture around 1400 that came to be known as the Renaissance. The splendor of the court came to be seen as a reflection of the strength of the ruler. Eventually, this idea spread northward to France.

The French Influence

At the same time that the French court was growing in wealth, opulence, and influence, England was mired in a thirty-year struggle known to historians as the Wars of the Roses. During the conflict, various nobles on whichever side was losing at the

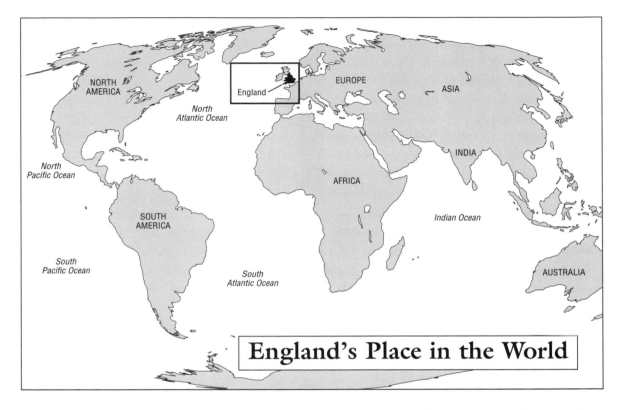

England's Place in the World

time would take refuge in France. Among them was Henry Tudor, earl of Richmond, destined to be King Henry VII, grandfather of Queen Elizabeth I.

Henry was able to see that the appearance of wealth and power was almost as important as wealth and power themselves. He also saw how important it was for a king to make himself the absolute center of power and to make sure that the power of each great noble amounted only to that given to him by the king.

When Henry became king in 1485 he was able to put his observations into practice, something his predecessors could not have done. The various dukes and earls had been too powerful in the past,

sometimes combining to overthrow a king. These nobles, however, had largely been killed off during the wars. Their places were taken by men dependent on Henry. Unlike English kings before him, Henry kept his leading nobles close around him—not only to serve him, but also so he could keep an eye on them.

As a result, the English royal court grew both in size and splendor. Henry copied the fashions of France and surrounded himself with pomp and ceremony, rich furnishings, and costly apparel. He did not much care for such magnificence personally, but knew he had to project a strong image. His early biographer Sir Francis Bacon, who served in Elizabeth's

Privy, or private, Council, wrote, "He had nothing in him of vainglory, but yet kept state and majesty to the height, being sensible that majesty maketh people bow, but vainglory boweth them."[3]

Henry VIII, Henry's son, carried the magnificence of the court even further, and the tradition was carried on by his granddaughter Elizabeth. As a woman, however, she could not be the warrior king. Instead, she cultivated—deliberately or not—the image of herself as the Virgin Queen, almost as a goddess to be worshiped. Indeed, when pressed by her subjects to marry, she said, "I am already bound to a husband, which is the kingdom of England."[4] Throughout her long reign Elizabeth was determined to make her kingdom, as reflected in her court, outshine all others.

Gloriana

When Elizabeth said that her accession to the throne of England was God's doing, she probably meant every word. It must, indeed, have seemed a miracle to her. As tradition dictated, she would spend the night before her coronation in the Tower of London. Yet, just a few years earlier she had spent months there as a prisoner, not knowing if she would emerge alive.

That the Tudor dynasty itself had emerged in 1485 from the wreckage of the Wars of the Roses was something of a miracle. The struggle for the throne had been between two branches of the royal Plantagenet family—the house of Lancaster and the house of York. At the final battle at Bosworth Field in 1485, the Lancastrians, led by Henry Tudor, earl of Richmond, at last prevailed. The Yorkist leader, King Richard III, was killed and his naked body thrown ignominiously across the back of a horse. A Lancastrian noble picked up the fallen monarch's crown and placed it on Henry's head.

King Henry VII's claim to that crown was slim at best. The Tudors' rise to prominence began when Owen, a Welsh adventurer who fought for England in the Hundred Years' War against France earlier in the 1400s, had the good fortune to marry Catherine, daughter of the king of France and widow of King Henry V of England.

Owen's son Edmund was made earl of Richmond and also married well, wedding

Margaret Beaufort. The Beauforts were descended from John of Gaunt, a son of King Edward III, and his mistress Katherine Swynford. When John's wife died, he married Katherine and succeeded in having their children declared legitimate.

An Unsteady Dynasty

Henry's claim, then, rested on the fact that he was the great-great-grandson of King Edward III through his grandmother, Margaret Beaufort, whose father had been born illegitimate. Immediately after becoming king, Henry VII sought to strengthen his position by marrying Elizabeth of York, widow of King Edward IV. The weakness of the Tudor claim, however, would make Henry and his descendants, including Elizabeth, lash out at anything or anyone that seemed to threaten their right to rule.

The new king considered it important to have a luxurious court to strengthen his image, but he hated to spend money, a trait Elizabeth would share. Henry had spent much of the Wars of the Roses as an impoverished refugee in France. When he became king, the treasury of England had been virtually emptied by the cost of the war. As a result, Henry constantly sought to increase his income through taxes and fines and, over the course of his reign, was successful in rebuilding the royal wealth.

His son, King Henry VIII, had none of his father's aversion to spending money. He sought a reputation as a great military leader and thus involved England in numerous and costly foreign wars. He tried mightily—and expensively—to outshine his French rival, King Francis I. When the kings met for negotiations near the French port of Calais in 1520, Henry's tent city covered two and a half acres and featured a fountain that spouted not only water, but also two kinds of wine. The sumptuousness of both camps was such that the meeting came to be known as the Field of Cloth of Gold.

Thanks to his father's thrift, Henry VIII had money to spend. What he lacked was a male heir. Henry's first wife, the Spanish princess Catherine of Aragon,

Unlike his frugal father, King Henry VIII spent money with abandon.

gave birth to a daughter, Mary, in 1516, but it eventually became clear that she would bear no more children. England had never been ruled by a woman, and Henry considered the notion dangerous, reasoning that a queen would be dominated by her husband, who just might be a foreign prince.

Anne Boleyn

Meanwhile, Henry had fallen in love with Anne Boleyn, a young woman at court. He tried to make her his mistress, but she refused him, insisting on marriage. The love-struck king agreed and in 1527 set out to have his marriage to Catherine annulled—that is, officially declared invalid.

The only person who could annul the marriage of the king of England and a princess of Spain was Pope Clement VII, head of the Roman Catholic Church. Normally, this would not have been a problem. Clement, however, was a virtual prisoner of the Holy Roman Emperor, Charles V, whose army held Rome. Charles was Catherine's nephew, and the pope dared not antagonize him by granting Henry's request.

What those around the king referred to as his "great matter" dragged on for almost six years. Henry pulled every diplomatic string possible, but was unable to obtain an annulment. Finally his chief adviser, Thomas Cromwell, found a solution. Henry would proclaim a Church of England, separate from Rome, with himself at the head.

In April 1533 Parliament, England's legislative body, passed the Act of Restraint of Appeals, severing all of the nation's ties with the Roman Catholic Church. A month later Archbishop of Canterbury Thomas Cranmer, now the highest-ranking clergyman in the country, obligingly declared Henry's marriage to Catherine null and void.

Henry had not waited for such a decree. He and Anne Boleyn had been married in a secret ceremony in January. By the time Anne was crowned queen on June 1 she was noticeably pregnant. Astrologers consulted the stars and assured Henry the child would be the long-awaited prince. So did the royal physicians. The king, thus encouraged, resolved to name the baby either Henry or Edward.

A New Princess

Anne's baby was born on the afternoon of September 7, 1533, in the royal palace at Greenwich. To the great disappointment of Henry and Anne—and the great dismay of the astrologers and doctors—it was a girl. She was named Elizabeth after her grandmother, Elizabeth of York.

Henry hid his frustration as best he could. In a ceremony as elaborate as he could make it, the baby girl was christened "the right high, right noble, and right excellent Princess Elizabeth."[5] The next year, Parliament passed the Act of Succession rendering Princess Mary illegitimate and making the new princess heir to the throne.

Queen Elizabeth's mother, Anne Boleyn, was unable to produce a son, much to the displeasure of her husband, Henry VIII.

Still, Henry was determined to have a son. His hopes rose when Anne again became pregnant, but early in 1536 the baby—a boy—was stillborn. The king was convinced it was a judgment from God for his having divorced Catherine, who had died a few weeks earlier, and that Anne would never bear a son. Furthermore, his roving eye had settled on one of Anne's ladies-in-waiting, Jane Seymour.

Cromwell again smoothed the way for his royal master. He produced evidence—most of it very flimsy—that Anne had committed adultery, which because of her position as queen would have con-

stituted treason. She strongly denied the charge, but to no avail. She was arrested and sent to the Tower of London. There, on May 19, 1536, she was beheaded. Eleven days later, Henry and Jane Seymour were married. Sixteen months later Henry finally had a son, whom he named Edward.

Since Elizabeth very rarely spoke about her mother in later years, it is impossible to know how aware she had been, at age four, of what had happened. She probably sensed that her status had changed. She was no longer addressed as your highness, but Lady Elizabeth. Fewer people waited on her and they were not as respectful as before.

Her Father's Daughter

The baby prince was declared Henry's heir, and Elizabeth was pronounced illegitimate. Rumors spread that she was not even Henry's daughter, but that of one of Anne's supposed lovers. No one who saw the child, however, could doubt that Henry was her father. She had the same pale skin and red hair and later the same commanding presence and hair-trigger temper. One foreign ambassador would describe her as "pleasing rather than beautiful,"[6] although to her face those around her praised her beauty at every opportunity.

Elizabeth's childhood, while not exactly happy, certainly was not miserable. King Henry treated her with genuine affection and she, in turn, cared very much for him, whatever she might have known about what he had done to her mother. She spent much of her time with young Edward, whom she loved, and took advantage of the superb tutoring of the noted scholar Roger of Ascham. She learned French, Latin, Greek, and Italian and studied history, philosophy, and theology.

Even when she was quite young, childhood seemed to have passed Elizabeth by. People remarked on how solemn she appeared. Edmund Bohun, a contemporary historian, wrote that she "was adorned with more than usual maiden modesty."[7] She watched everything around her carefully and seldom displayed her emotions. One observer said she seemed more like a man of forty than a child of six.

Henry VIII died in 1547 and the eleven-year-old Edward became king. Elizabeth lived in the household of Catherine Parr, Henry's sixth and last wife, who treated her with kindness. Also in Catherine's household, however, was her second husband, Thomas Seymour, whom she had married after the king's death. Seymour was King Edward's uncle and the younger brother of the duke of Somerset, Lord Protector of the young king and the most powerful man in England.

Flirting with Scandal

Thomas Seymour was more affectionate toward the teenaged Elizabeth than was proper. He would burst into her bedroom, dressed only in his nightshirt, throw back her covers, and attempt to tickle her. His wife sometimes participated in these games, but after she found the pair embracing one morning, Elizabeth was sent away.

Catherine died in 1549 and Thomas Seymour, jealous of his brother's position, hatched a plan to marry Elizabeth and rule England through her. His plot was discovered, however, and Thomas Seymour was arrested for treason. The duke of Somerset suspected Elizabeth of being part of the plan, but the fifteen-year-old girl remained steadfast and calm under repeated questioning.

At one point, Elizabeth's enemies said she was pregnant with Thomas Seymour's child. She met the challenge head-on, writing to the Lord Protector demanding that she be allowed to come to court "that I may show myself there as I am."[8] Thomas Seymour was found guilty of treason and beheaded. When Elizabeth was informed, she did not break down, as her enemies undoubtedly hoped, but said only, "This day died a man with much wit and very little judgment."[9]

King Edward died in 1553, probably of tuberculosis, and, despite having been declared illegitimate, his half sister Mary became queen. A devout Catholic, she returned England to the authority of the Roman church and married King Philip II of Spain. However, because Protestantism—the doctrine opposed to many of the beliefs and practices of the Catholic Church—had taken firm hold in England, Mary and her marriage were highly unpopular.

An Eloquent Defense

In 1549, Princess Elizabeth, then fifteen years old, was accused by Edward Seymour, Lord Protector for the young King Edward VII, of conspiring with Seymour's brother Thomas to seize the throne. To answer the charge and rumors that she was pregnant with Thomas Seymour's child, Elizabeth wrote an eloquent letter in her defense, this excerpt of which is found in The Private Character of Queen Elizabeth *by Frederick Chamberlin.*

These be the Things which I both declared to Master Tyrwhit [her interrogator], and also whereof my Conscience beareth me Witness, which I would not for all earthly Things offend in any Thing: for I know that I have a Soul to save, as well as other Folks have, wherefore I will above all Things have Respect unto this same. If there be any more Things which I can remember, I will either write it myself, or cause Master Tyrwhit to write it. Master Tyrwhit and others have told me that there goeth rumours Abroad which be greatly both against my Honor and Honestie (which above all other things I esteem), which be these; that I am in the Tower; and with Child by My Lord Admiral [Thomas Seymour]. My Lord, these are shameful Schandlers, for the which, besides the great Desire I have to see the King's Majestie [Edward VI], I shall most heartily desire your Lordship that I may come to the Court after your first Determination; that I may show myself there as I am. Written in haste, from Hatfield this 28th of January.

Dangerous Times

These were dangerous years for Elizabeth. Her religious views were distinctly Protestant as a result of her upbringing and the influence of Catherine Parr. Nevertheless, she was careful to conform—outwardly, at least—to her half sister's religion. Even so, there were several Protestant plots to re-move Mary from the throne and replace her with Elizabeth.

Elizabeth doubtless knew of, or at least suspected, these schemes, but refused to take part in what was a dangerous and perhaps deadly game.

Cautious though she was, Elizabeth could not help getting caught up in the political intrigue of the time. When a rebellion by an English officer, Sir Thomas Wyatt, was crushed, Mary's councillors claimed Elizabeth had supported it. They viewed her as a threat and thought Mary would be more secure if Elizabeth were executed.

Elizabeth was arrested and repeatedly questioned. She refused to confess and was sent to the Tower of London. Elizabeth was frantic, afraid that she would share the fate of her mother, Anne Boleyn. She spent two months in the Tower, but her enemies still could find no proof of her guilt. Later, still a prisoner, she was moved to the royal palace at Woodstock. There, in her room, she used a diamond ring to scratch on a window pane,

> Much suspected by me
> Nothing proved can be,
> Quoth Elizabeth, prisoner.[10]

Elizabeth continued to walk a political tightrope throughout Mary's reign. She gave no encouragement to Protestants who wanted to make her queen. At the same time she skillfully avoided Philip's attempts to marry her off to a foreign Catholic prince. As it became evident that Mary would not have children and that Elizabeth would be the next ruler, more and more nobles gave her their promises of support.

Mary's Final Months

Mary's final months were full of disappointments. She thought herself pregnant, but it turned out to be a tumor—probably ovarian cancer—that would

Princess Elizabeth is held as a prisoner in the Tower of London at the decree of her half sister, Queen Mary.

"A Calm and Quiet Season"

After the religious strife and foreign wars of Queen Mary I's reign, the people of England welcomed the changes they thought Queen Elizabeth I would bring. Raphael Holinshed, a contemporary historian, gave this view, found in A Portrait of Elizabeth I, *edited by Roger Pringle, in his account of the new queen's entry into London in 1558.*

After all the stormy, tempestuous, and blustering windy weather of Queen Mary was overblown, the darksome clouds of discomfort dispersed, the palpable fogs and mists of most intolerable misery consumed, and the dashing showers of persecution overpast, it pleased God to send England a calm and quiet season, a clear and lovely sunshine . . . and a world of blessings by good Queen Elizabeth, into whose gracious reign we are now to make a happy entrance as followeth. . . . At her entering the city, she was of the people received marvelous entirely, as appeared by the assemblies, prayers, wishes, welcomings, cries, tender words and all other signs, which argued a wonderful earnest love of most obedient subjects toward their sovereign. And on the other side, her grace, by holding up her hands and merry countenance to such as stood far off, and most tender and gentle language to those that stood nigh unto her grace, did declare herself no less thankfully to receive her people's good will, than they lovingly offered it to her.

eventually kill her. Her husband Philip, frustrated at her inability to produce an heir, abandoned her and, indeed, began paying more attention to Elizabeth. Finally, Mary realized that her dream of returning England to Catholicism would end with her death. In her bitterness, she increased the persecutions of Protestants. More than three hundred were burned at the stake during her reign, earning her the nickname "Bloody Mary."

Mary died on November 17, 1588. To the Protestants, who made up the large majority of English, her death was a deliverance and Elizabeth was the deliverer. Mary had persecuted Protestants to the very last, with six people executed less than a week before her death. People would later sing, "Six days after these were burned to death / God sent us our Elizabeth."[11]

Indeed, it must have seemed to the people of England that dark clouds had given way to brilliant sunshine. As the young queen rode into London on November 28, cheering crowds lined the streets. Choirs sang. Cannons roared forth a greeting. When the procession reached the Tower of London, where new rulers traditionally stayed until their formal coronation, Elizabeth fell to her knees, saying, "Some have fallen from being princes of this land to prisoners in this place. I am raised from being a prisoner in this place to be a prince of this land."[12]

The Coronation

The coronation took place on January 15, 1559. On the previous day, Elizabeth had taken the "Recognition Procession" the short distance from the Tower to Westminster, where she would be crowned. Even though the royal treasury had been depleted by Mary to support Philip's wars, Elizabeth was determined to begin her reign on a grand scale. She knew, as her father and grandfather had, the importance of outward splendor to awe both her subjects and also the foreign ambassadors who would report what they saw to their own rulers.

What they saw was a young woman of twenty-five clothed in a dress made from a golden fabric and wearing an ermine cape about her shoulders. She wore a circlet of gold on her forehead, and her auburn hair, flowing loose in the style of an unmarried woman, framed a pale, oval face. She sat in a chariot draped with red velvet. Four knights walked surrounding her, holding a golden canopy over her head.

Several times she halted the procession so that someone—here an old man, there a child—could approach and speak to her. A humbly dressed woman offered her a sprig of rosemary. She accepted it with thanks and held it in her lap the remainder of the way. Her resemblance to her father was so strong that at one point along the way a voice shouted, "Remember old King Henry the Eighth."[13] Elizabeth responded with a dazzling smile.

Elizabeth showed she was a born politician. She instinctively knew how to appeal to her people and win their affection. A witness to the procession, Sir John Hayward, wrote, "If ever any person had either the gift or the style to win the hearts of people, it was this Queen, and if ever she did express the same it was at that present, in coupling mildness with majesty as she did, and in stately stooping to the meanest sort. All her faculties were in motion, and every motion seemed a well-guided action."[14]

The people loved her, and she loved them in return. To them, she was like a goddess sent to watch over them. Her qualities—beauty, majesty, virtue, wisdom—were to be described by the poet Edmund Spenser in his epic *The Fairie Queene,* which would give her a name by which she would be known to her subjects and to history—Gloriana.

The Human Touch

Yet, Elizabeth had the capacity to be divine and human at the same time. She might rule the people of England, but she was one of them and neither she nor they ever forgot it. One morning, after she had changed her mind repeatedly about leaving for a journey, the frustrat-

Elizabeth I was a forceful and charismatic queen. Her influence on friends and enemies alike was significant.

ed driver of a wagon in the courtyard below her chamber said, "Now I see that the Queen is a woman [just like] my wife."[15] Elizabeth's reaction was typical of her style. She leaned out the window, calling the man a villain, but threw some coins to him as well.

The queen took her responsibilities seriously, telling her councillors, "Have a care over my people. . . . See unto them. See unto them, for they are my charge [duty]. I charge you, even as God hath charged me . . . my care is for my people."[16] During the recognition procession, she stood at one point and cried out to the people, "Be ye ensured, that I will be as good unto you as ever queen was to her people. No will in me

can lack, neither do I trust shall there lack any power. And persuade yourselves, that for the safety and quietness [peace] of you all, I will not spare, if need be, to spend my blood. God thank you all."[17]

Queen and Court

The reign of Queen Elizabeth I had begun in splendor and would continue in that mode for another forty-seven years. She would dazzle her subjects, her allies, and her enemies with the grandeur of her court and the force of her personality. The Elizabethan court would become very much a reflection of the queen herself—confident, secure in majesty, obsessed with luxury—moving through the difficulties she and her nation faced with a bold swagger.

Elizabeth's court was destined to be one of the last of its kind. The time was approaching when monarchs no longer would be able to make their courts the focus of their kingdoms, the central point from which all things and all people were ruled. The voice of the common people was growing stronger, and kings and queens would eventually have to share their power with elected representatives.

In 1559, however, that day still lay in the future. The kingdom of England was centered on the court, and the court was centered on Elizabeth. As one modern writer put it, Elizabeth "was essentially the last of the great English medieval monarchs, the last of the nation's rulers to control the kingdom by sheer force of personality and unchallenged authority."[18]

Chapter 2

The Queen's Majesty

Elizabeth was a born actress, and the court was the stage on which she played the great productions—both comedies and tragedies—of her reign. But, every actor needs a supporting cast and audience, and both roles were filled by the attendants, courtiers, servants, and hangers-on who swarmed about the queen wherever she was. They were there either to serve Elizabeth or to serve those who served her—and in so doing to serve their own interests as well.

The court expanded in ever-widening circles from a central focal point—the queen. Closest to her were the women who attended her most intimate needs, such as bathing and dressing. Then came the Maids of Honor, who accompanied her almost everywhere. Immediately outside the female circle were the grooms of the Privy Chamber, gentlemen pensioners, members of the Privy Council, and so forth, finally reaching those courtiers on the outskirts who were looking for a way inside.

For the most part, the inner circle of the court was made up of members of the most noble families in England. Thus, while they held titles that described a particular service—Mistress of the Robes, Master of the Horse—they seldom actually did the work implied by the titles. That was done by an army of butlers, maids, cooks, dressmakers, grooms, laundresses, and other servants. In addition, there were the musicians to entertain the court, the soldiers to guard it, and the clergymen to pray over it. Altogether, about fifteen hundred people made up the court of Elizabeth I.

The Three Chambers

The court was both a social institution and a physical place. In earlier centuries, it had consisted of a single chamber in which the king slept, ate, and conducted affairs of state. During the 1400s the one large chamber was replaced with three—the outer or Guard Chamber where those seeking an audience first came, the Presence Chamber where the king sat throned to receive visitors, and the Privy Chamber, which consisted of the king's private living quarters.

Elizabeth's grandfather, Henry VII, divided the Privy Chamber from the more formal areas of the court and provided it with a separate staff. Those who served Henry VII personally were not nobles, but, as Italian observer Baldassare Castiglione wrote a few years later, "persons of little worth except in the matter of knowing how to give good personal service."[19] This practice changed under Henry VIII, and members of the nobility assumed some very ignoble titles. The Groom of the Stool, for instance, officially had the job of emptying the king's close-stool, or toilet.

The transition of the court from Mary to Elizabeth was far easier than it had been from Edward VI to Mary. Mary had inherited a staff made up almost entirely of men and, of course, needed a female staff for personal service. Under the kings, many men were members of both the Privy Chamber and the Privy Council, the king's closest advisers. Starting with Mary and continuing under Elizabeth, the Privy Chamber, consisting mostly of women, took on a purely domestic instead of administrative role.

Queen Elizabeth's grandfather, Henry VII, was the first English monarch to separate his private living quarters from the areas where official business was conducted.

The Queen's Women

The women who served Elizabeth did so at four levels—Ladies of the Bedchamber, Gentlewomen of the Privy Chamber, Maids of Honor, and Chamberers. There were usually four Ladies of the Bedchamber. These women, many of them older and married, were the queen's closest friends. Catherine Ashley, who had been appointed Elizabeth's governess when she was four years old, was among the first group. So was Blanche Parry, who had been in the queen's household even longer, and Elizabeth's first cousin Catherine Knollys, daughter of Anne Boleyn's sister Mary.

Ashley served as the first head of the Privy Chamber staff with the title of Chief Gentlewoman. The other Gentlewomen held titles dealing with specific responsibilities. Parry was Keeper of the Royal Books, and Knollys was Mistress of the Robes.

The Gentlewomen of the Privy Chamber ranked next. These eight women were also of noble birth but were usually not as intimate with the queen as the Ladies of the Bedchamber. Some had specific duties such as the Keeper of the Plate—"plate" meaning not only dishes but also other forms of precious metal. Others appeared to have no responsibilities but to wait on the queen.

Most of the responsibility for running the household fell on the four Chamberers. They were usually not from the nobility, but were chosen for their ability to direct the work of the servants. Their duties included storing linen, plate, and a wide variety of other household items.

The Ladies of the Bedchamber, Gentlewomen of the Privy Chamber, and Chamberers were paid annual salaries. Most were extraordinarily loyal and remained in Elizabeth's service until their deaths. One Gentlewoman, Dorothy Edmonds, served the entire forty-five years of the reign. Indeed, a total of only twenty-eight women served in the sixteen salaried posts during this time.

Maids of Honor

The Maids of Honor, usually six to eight in number, were more ornamental than functional. They were young, beautiful, unmarried, and were drawn from the noblest families of England. Beauty, however, was far from the only qualification. Elizabeth was highly intelligent, well educated, and cultured. She had no wish to be in the company of fools. The Maids of Honor, therefore, had to have brains as well as beauty and were expected to have talents as well, such as sewing or playing musical instruments.

The Maids of Honor accompanied the queen almost everywhere she went. Arrayed beside and behind Elizabeth as she held court, they acted as a backdrop against which she displayed herself to best advantage. In the middle years of her reign, for example, when Elizabeth favored black dresses, the Maids of Honor would wear silver and white.

The Role of Men

There were fewer men on the staff. The Gentlemen of the Privy Chamber ranked highest, and only two men were to hold this post—John Ashley, husband of Catherine Ashley, and Sir Christopher Hatton. They had no definable duties, but were expected to be on call when needed by the queen. When she needed more than one or two male attendants, there were a number of unpaid courtiers available who were always eager for a chance to make an impression on the queen.

There also were six Grooms of the Privy Chamber, either trusted attendants from Elizabeth's previous households or bright young men from good families. They had various jobs associated with keeping the queen's apartments in order—everything from arranging for firewood to mending clocks. Elizabeth also frequently used them as messengers.

As a Gentleman of the Privy Chamber, Sir Christopher Hatton was expected to be always at Queen Elizabeth's beck and call.

The other Privy Chamber office was that of the Gentleman Usher. This official was very important to Elizabeth because he controlled who could enter the Presence Chamber. She trusted him to keep out those who were in her disfavor or anyone she did not want to see for some reason.

Many more positions dealt with matters beyond the Privy Chamber, and some were among the most important at court. The Lord Chamberlain had the overall responsibility of running the entire household, not just that of the queen. The Lord Chamberlain had considerable power because he determined who could and could not live at court. He also was in charge of all entertainments, although these were actually arranged by another officer, the Master of Revels. Other high-ranking posts, some of which carried only ceremonial duties, included the Master of Horse, Lord Steward, Chief Butler, Captain of the Guard, and Treasurer of the Chamber.

Pomp and Ceremony

The queen and members of the court carried out their day-to-day activities with the utmost pomp and ceremony. The mealtime pageantry, for instance, started with two ushers entering the hall, kneeling three times before the empty table before setting the cloth. Others followed and, after kneeling, placed salt, bread, and plates on the table. Two of the queen's ladies, also after deep curtsies, then rubbed the plates with the bread and salt, tokens of prosperity. Twenty-four guardsmen then carried in the food on golden dishes, after being given a mouthful each to test for poison.

At last, all was ready, but Elizabeth herself was almost never there. Instead, her Maids of Honor would serve her plate and take it to a private room where she ate, usually from no more than three or four of the dishes. She would appear, however, at state banquets.

The ceremony was equally elaborate each time the queen went out in public. A French ambassador wrote in his report that

> when the Queen goes abroad in public the Lord Chamberlain walks first, being followed by all the nobility who are in Court, and the Knights of the Order [of the Garter] walk after, near the Queen's person. . . . After come the six heralds who bear maces before the Queen. After her march the fifty Gentlemen of the Guard, each carrying a halberd [combination battle-ax and pike], and sumptuously attired; and after that the Maids and Ladies who accompany them very well attired.[20]

A Frugal Queen

Such displays were costly, and Elizabeth, notoriously tightfisted, bore the expense grudgingly. Once, when told the cost of running the household, she thundered, "I will

Ode to Elizabeth

The Faerie Queene by Edmund Spenser is considered by many experts the next great poem to have been written in English after Chaucer's Canterbury Tales. Spenser wrote the epic piece, full of references to mythology, in honor of Queen Elizabeth, and the fairy queen's name, Gloriana, was one of many used for Elizabeth during her reign. This excerpt is found in A Portrait of Elizabeth I, edited by Roger Pringle.

All over her a cloth of state was spread,
Not of rich tissue nor of cloth of gold,
Nor of aught else that may be richest red,
But like a cloud, as likest may be told,
   that her broad spreading wings did wide unfold;
Whose skirts were bordered with bright sunny beams,
Glistering like gold, amongst the plights [folds] enrolled,
And here and there shooting forth silver streams,
'Mongst which crept little angels through the glittering gleams. . . .

Thus she did sit in sovereign majesty,
Holding a scepter in her royal hand,
The sacred pledge of peace and clemency,
With which high God had blessed her happy land,
Maugre [despite] so many foes which did withstand.
But at her feet her sword was likewise laid,
Whose long rest rusted the bright steely brand:
Yet when as foes enforced, or friends sought aid,
She could it sternly draw, that all the world dismayed.

not suffer the dishonourable spoil and increase that no prince before me did to the offence of God and the great grievance of my loving subjects."[21]

She loved, however, for people to spend money on her. She gave all members of the court presents of plate at New Year's, in amounts carefully measured according to the recipient's status. The courtiers, in return, were expected to give the queen presents worth more than what they received. In 1562, these gifts ranged from a silver writing set adorned with pearls from Sir William Cecil to a mince pie from baker John Betts. The total value was £1,262, or about $190,000 in modern terms.

Elizabeth also received presents on Accession Day each November 17, the day her reign had begun. She probably enjoyed Accession Day more than New Year's because the holiday was solely in her honor and she did not have to give presents, only receive them.

Elizabeth loved to receive flattery almost as much as she enjoyed being given presents. She never tired of people praising her wisdom, dancing, learning, and—most of all—her beauty. She shamelessly fished for compliments and seldom failed to catch them. For example, when she coyly asked one ambassador if he thought her Maids of Honor were beautiful, he said he was unable "to judge the stars in the presence of the sun."[22] The queen was delighted.

She continued to accept praise of her beauty long after it had faded. Sir Robert

Although a highly competent ruler, Elizabeth was vain and susceptible to flattery.

Cecil, her principal secretary in the final years, claimed that "time, which catcheth everybody, leaves only you untouched."[23]

The Royal Image

Elizabeth knew better, but did her best to keep the ravages of time at a distance. Official portraits had to conform to a standard that showed her much younger than she actually was. During the last twenty years of her reign, she banned all mirrors from her private quarters as "so farre from all niceness."[24] The young Maids of Honor, however, loved mirrors and rather than give them up, hastened to hide them whenever the queen came through their quarters. Eventually, even Elizabeth had to concede defeat in her battle against time. A few weeks before she died, she commanded a mirror be brought to her. She gazed for a moment at the reflection of a wrinkled old woman and then cursed those who had flattered her all those years.

The flattery, of course, had a purpose. It was a way to get the queen to agree to something someone wanted, but it did not always work. Elizabeth was wise enough to see the purpose behind the fair words. She once told a foreign ambassador that her councillors "deal with me like physicians who administering a drug, make it more acceptable by giving it a good aromatical savour or when they give pills to gild them all over."[25]

If courtiers were not close enough to the queen to use flattery to get what they

A Royal Procession

Paul Hentzner, a German visitor, watched Queen Elizabeth I and her attendants process through the halls of Greenwich Palace on a Sunday morning in 1598. He wrote an account of the sight, this excerpt of which is found in Gloriana's Glass, *edited by Alan Glover.*

First went the gentlemen, barons, earls, knights of the garter, all richly dressed and bare-headed; next came the chancellor, bearing the seals in a red-silk purse, between two; one of which carried the royal scepter, the other the sword of state, in a red scabbard, studded with golden fleurs de lis [the French symbol of royalty], the point upwards: next came the queen, in the sixty-fifth year of her age, as we were told, very majestic; her face oblong, fair, but wrinkled; her eyes small, yet black and pleasant; her nose a little hooked; her lips narrow, and her teeth black; (a defect the English seem subject to, from their too great use of sugar) she had in her ears two pearls, with very rich drops; she wore false hair, and that red; upon her head she had a small crown reported to be made of some of the gold of the celebrated Lunebourg table. . . . As she went along in all this state and magnificence, she spoke very graciously, first to one, then to another, whether foreign ministers, or those who attended her for different reasons, in English, French, and Italian. . . . The ladies of the court followed next to her, very handsome and well shaped, and for the most part dressed in white; she was guarded on each side by the gentlemen pensioners, fifty in number, with gilt battleaxes.

wanted, they might employ someone closer who could put in a good word for them. Such intercession did not come cheap, and the closer to the queen a person was, the higher price they could charge for their help. None were closer to her than the women of the Privy Chamber, and their services could be expensive. But, while Sir Walter Raleigh might complain that the queen's women were "like witches, capable of doing great harm but no good,"[26] men sought their services nevertheless.

A Case of Bribery

In 1595, for instance, an attorney, Anthony Bacon, sought a royal pardon for a client. Dorothy Edmonds, a Gentlewoman of the Chamber since the start of the reign, was approached and offered £100 ($15,000). She initially agreed to put the case before the queen, provided the Lord Chamberlain agreed to let her do so. After consulting the Lord Chamberlain, however, she reported to Bacon that she had been advised to accept no less than £1,000.

Bacon was trapped. He could not refuse Lady Edmonds's price and go elsewhere. If he did, she would speak against his client to Elizabeth. Bacon paid up, but complained about the "ruffianry" of women who "presume thus to grange and huck [collect and barter] causes."[27]

While Elizabeth could be influenced, she certainly was no pawn in the hands of the members of her court. No one, however close to her, could be assured

of getting a wish granted. Indeed, her mood swings were extreme, making her totally unpredictable. Her godson, Sir John Harrington, wrote, "When she smiled, it had a pure sunshine that every one did choose to bask in if they could; but anon came a sudden gathering of clouds, and the thunder fell in a wondrous manner on all."[28]

Elizabeth's Courage

Yet Elizabeth was not simply a monarch whose whims had to be endured. She was genuinely admired by those who served her, not only for her charm but also for her considerable personal courage. In 1587, when England was threatened by

As she aged, Elizabeth worked to maintain her royal bearing and powerful image.

Robert Dudley, the earl of Leicester, was a favorite of the queen and became wealthy through royal favors.

an invasion from Spain, she put on armor to address her troops. "I know I have the weak and feeble body of a woman," she said, "but I have the heart and stomach of a king."[29] On another occasion, when the followers of the earl of Essex tried to mount a rebellion against her in London, Elizabeth had to be talked out of going to confront them in person.

However much they loved her, most of the people who made up Elizabeth's court hoped, through their service, to be richly rewarded. Some were. While Elizabeth did not like to part with money, she could bestow noble titles and the lands that went with them. Even more profitable were the monopolies she could grant. For example, Robert Dudley, earl of Leicester, grew rich after being given the exclusive right to mine tin in the county of Cornwall. Likewise, the queen granted Sir Walter Raleigh the right to license all taverns selling imported sweet wine.

Service Unrewarded

Other courtiers were not so fortunate. Many served faithfully for years, only to receive nothing more than an annual New Year's present worth far less than the one they gave. Sir Henry Sidney served Elizabeth for twenty difficult years in rebellious Ireland. When he retired, however, he was heavily in debt and had "not so much land as would graze a mutton [single sheep]."[30]

The court of Elizabeth I, therefore, was a place of great culture, romance, and magnificence, but it could also be a snake pit of corruption, intrigue, and treachery. Moreover, while those in the queen's inner circle might live a life of luxury, those on the edges had to find their places as best they could, jostling one another for living space and for a chance to advance. Harrington, despite his favored position as Elizabeth's godson, found little noble about court life, which he termed "ill breeding with ill feedinge, and no love but that of the lustie god of gallantry."[31] And the perceptive Raleigh, contrasting the outward splendor of the court with its undercurrent of sleaze, wrote, "Say to the court, it glows/and shines like rotten wood."[32]

All the Queen's Men

Although Elizabeth I ruled in what was essentially a man's world, she dominated the men of her court. Sometimes she did so by sheer force of personality, as a king might have, but she could be more subtle—flirting and flattering, taunting and teasing, employing smiles and tears. She loved men, but gave her heart to none. She played them off against each other, favoring one to arouse the jealousy of another. One of her favorites, Sir Christopher Hatton, said, "The Queen did fish for men's souls, and had so sweet a bait that no-one could escape from her net-work."[33]

And, once she had ensnared the men of the court, Elizabeth was reluctant to let them go. She wanted them close to her, both emotionally and physically. She hated the idea of them being married, and single men had a much better chance of gaining and keeping her favor. She enjoyed hearing them praise her beauty and profess their undying love.

War's Wastes

One of the reasons she despised wars—besides the fact that they cost money—was that her dashing young men were eager to dash away to fight—and possibly die—for glory. She was grief stricken when Sir Philip Sidney, her favorite poet as well as her ceremonial cupbearer, was killed while fighting in the Netherlands. Years later, when another favorite, Sir Charles Blount, joined her troops abroad without permission, Elizabeth ordered him back. When he arrived, she scolded him, invoking the memory of her lost poet by saying, "Serve me so once more, and I will lay you fast enough for running. You will never leave it [war] until you are knocked on the head, as that inconsiderate fellow Sidney was. You shall go when I send you, and in the meantime see that you lodge in the Court, where you may follow your book, read and discourse of the wars."[34]

Thus it was that many a courtier who yearned to prove his manhood fighting for the queen spent his time instead entertaining her and her ladies. Some were made knights by the queen, but it was for courtly accomplishments rather than military valor. These were derisively called "carpet knights" by veteran soldiers because they knelt on a carpet to receive knighthood instead of winning it on the battlefield.

Elizabeth had another reason for keeping her chief nobles at court. She wanted to be able to keep her eye on them, a policy that had served her father and grandfather well. She much preferred keeping them close and watching them vie with one another for her attention

The Queen's Council

To rule England, Queen Elizabeth I depended on the wisdom and advice of the men who made up the Privy Council. Throughout most of her reign, the two most prominent councillors were Robert Dudley and William Cecil. The ambassador from Spain gave this unflattering description of the two men. It is found in A Portrait of Elizabeth I, *edited by Roger Pringle.*

The principal person in the Council at present is William Cecil, now Lord Burley, a knight of the garter. He is a man of mean sort, but very astute, false, lying, and full of artifice. He is a great heretic [Protestant] and such a clownish Englishman as to believe that all the Christian princes joined together are not able to injure the sovereign of his country . . . and, by means of his vigilance and craftiness, together with his utter unscrupulousness of word and deed, thinks to outwit the ministers of other princes. This to a certain extent he has hitherto succeeded in doing. Next after him, the man who has most to do with affairs is Robert Dudley, earl of Leicester, not that he is fit for such work, but because of the great favour with which the Queen regards him. He is a light and greedy man who maintains the robbers and lives by their plunder.

rather than having them far away on their own lands, perhaps forming alliances against her.

Dudley

The principal men in Elizabeth's life during her reign fell into two categories—those who sought to marry her and those on whom she depended to run the government. One man, Robert Dudley, was prominent in both groups. He and Elizabeth had known one another since childhood, and Dudley had been one of her most steadfast supporters during Mary's reign. At one point, when she had been in financial difficulty, he had sold some of his lands to help her.

There was no doubt that Elizabeth had great affection for the man she called my sweet Robin, but there were many barriers to their marriage. For one thing, Dudley was already married, having done so in 1550 when he was only seventeen years old. For another, he

Although a great friend of Elizabeth since childhood, Robert Dudley was not considered a suitable candidate for marriage to the queen.

had no royal ancestors and Elizabeth was extremely conscious of status. Third, Dudley had many enemies among the queen's most trusted councillors, including the earl of Sussex, who called him the Gypsy because of his dark complexion and considered him overly ambitious and untrustworthy.

The main obstacle, however, to Elizabeth's marriage to Dudley—or to anyone else—was her deep-seated aver-

sion to marriage itself. Dudley once told a friend that Elizabeth, when only eight years old, had said to him, "I shall never marry."[35] One could hardly blame her. She possibly, by that age, knew what marriage had ultimately meant to her mother, Anne Boleyn. Subsequent events would not have reassured her, either. She was to see her mother's fate befall Catherine Howard, Henry VIII's fourth wife, who was executed for adultery in

1542 and who had always befriended the young Princess Elizabeth. She was a first-hand witness to the marital misery of her half sister, Queen Mary. She also had additional reason to fear marriage when Catherine Parr, who had been like a mother to her, died in childbirth in 1548.

The Marriage Question

Despite the queen's aversion, the question in the eyes of England and the rest of Europe, however, was not if Elizabeth would marry, but whom. Women inherit-ing a throne were rare enough, but one ruling alone without a king was unheard of. She was expected, like Queen Mary, to marry and rule along with a husband and, as soon as possible, to produce an heir.

Elizabeth, however, had no wish to share her power with a husband or anyone else. Once, when Dudley dared argue with her, she screamed at him, "God's death, my Lord, I will have here one mistress but no master."[36] As a perceptive ambassador from Scotland told her, "I know your spirit cannot endure a commander."[37]

Elizabeth and Dudley

Robert Dudley, earl of Leicester, was probably the only man with whom Queen Elizabeth I was ever passionately in love. An ambassador from Scotland, Sir James Melville, observed how Dudley was treated by the queen and also was shown firsthand by her what Dudley meant to her. His description is found in A Portrait of Elizabeth I, *edited by Roger Pringle.*

I was required to stay [at court] till I should see him [Dudley] made Earl of Leicester and Baron of Denbigh; which was done at Westminster with great solemnity, the Queen herself helping to put on his ceremonial [robe], he sitting upon his knees before her with great gravity. But she could not refrain from putting her hand in his neck, smilingly tickling him, the French Ambassador and I standing by. . . .

She took me to her bed-chamber, and opened a little cabinet, wherein were divers little pictures wrapt within paper, and their names written with her own hand upon the papers. Upon the first that she took up was written, "My Lord's Picture." I held up the candle, and pressed to see that picture so named. She appeared loath to let me see it; yet my importunity prevailed for a sight thereof, and [I] found it to be the Earl of Leicester's picture.

No one, except possibly Dudley, thought that she would remain single. Certainly Parliament expected her to marry. Shortly after Elizabeth's coronation, Parliament sent a delegation to her, asking what her plans for marriage were and telling her how important Parliament considered it for her to wed quickly. The queen was gracious but firm. She chided Parliament—"whose duties are to obey" for intruding on the personal affairs of the queen—"them that may command."[38] As for marriage, she said, "I am attracted to spinsterhood not by prejudice, but rather by natural inclination. I call the wedding ring, the 'yoke ring.'"[39]

The Suitors

Nevertheless, she never—even well into middle age—ruled out marriage altogether. She knew that marriage with her was an enticing bauble to dangle in front of foreign princes who hoped to make England their allies. The first to try to snatch it was Philip II of Spain, her late sister's husband. Elizabeth had no intention of marrying Philip, but she put him off for months to the great frustration of the Spanish ambassador to England, who wrote to his master that "this country . . . has fallen into the hands of a woman who is the Daughter of the Devil!"[40]

Philip eventually chose to seek a wife elsewhere and instead suggested his nephew, Archduke Charles of Austria, as a husband for Elizabeth. Charles, however, had no better luck than Philip. Neither did Duke Casimir of the Palatine

in Germany, Prince Eric of Sweden, Duke William of Savoy, the French Duc de Nemours or Henry, duke of Anjou, brother of the king of France. Two Englishmen—the earl of Arundel and Sir William Pickering—were mentioned as possible husbands but got little encouragement. In fact, Pickering, after a long visit with Elizabeth, said he was sure she "meant to die a maid."[41]

Elizabeth seriously considered only two men as husbands. The first was Dudley. She favored her childhood friend above all other men in court. She made him her Master of Horse, and his bedchamber was next to hers in Whitehall Palace, which caused much speculation as to the nature of their relationship. She was constantly in his company and showered him with expensive gifts. Dudley, for his part, treated her with more familiarity than anyone else, even kissing her in public.

Fueling speculation was the fact that Dudley's wife, Amy, was in poor health. Most people at the court thought that, if and when she died, Dudley would marry Elizabeth and become king of England. Then in September 1560, after having sent all her servants to a nearby fair, Amy Dudley was found dead at the bottom of a staircase in her house near Oxford.

Rumors of Murder

The circumstances of Amy Dudley's death cast suspicion on her husband. The death was officially ruled a suicide—logical since Amy Dudley had been all but deserted by her husband and probably knew she was dying of breast cancer. Still, rumors circulated that she had been murdered. Her death, and Dudley's possible guilt, were the talk of England and of every court in Europe. In France, Elizabeth's cousin and rival, Mary, Queen of Scots, crowed, "The Queen of England is going to marry her Horsekeeper, who has killed his wife to make room for her."[42] There were more rumors. The Spanish ambassador wrote that Elizabeth had known of Amy Dudley's death before it happened.

Elizabeth reacted strongly, dismissing Dudley from court and thus ending his hopes, but the damage had been done. She knew that she could never marry him. To do so would cause such a scandal that she risked losing the goodwill of her people.

Even though Dudley was never to gain the ultimate prize, he remained Elizabeth's favorite. He even outlasted her wrath when he married her cousin, Lettice Knollys, without her knowledge. She created him earl of Leicester, and he continued to be one of the most influential men in England until his death in 1588. After Elizabeth's death, a note from Dudley was found in a jeweled casket she always kept by her bed. On it, in her handwriting, were the words "His Last Letter."

Alençon

If Dudley's being tall, handsome, and Elizabeth's exact age made him a likely candidate to be the queen's husband, her

The duke of Alençon was a charming but unattractive contender for the queen's hand. Elizabeth at first seemed receptive to the duke but later changed her mind.

other serious suitor, many years later, was an utterly unlikely one. Francois, duke of Alençon, was short, pockmarked, and twenty years younger than the queen he sought to marry. He was, however, very charming, and Elizabeth would be captivated by him. The match was proposed by the duke's mother, Catherine de Medici, who wanted her sons to rule both France and England, Francois's brother Henry having become king of France in 1574.

In addition to his charm, Alençon had some political advantages to recommend him. The people of Flanders, part of the Netherlands, had offered to make him their duke. From that position he could help the English drive the Spanish out of the Netherlands, where they were in position to possibly invade England. If he and Elizabeth were married, the Netherlands would be neither Spanish nor French, but English.

Elizabeth's Privy Council was divided. Cecil, her closest adviser, was for the marriage. Dudley was against it. Much of the country was against it as well. Alençon was a Catholic, and the people feared that such a marriage might bring back the religious strife that plagued England under Queen Mary.

Those who opposed the marriage had almost convinced Elizabeth when Alençon's envoy, Jean de Simier, played his strongest card. He had discovered what many at court knew—but had not told Elizabeth—that Robert Dudley had remarried, this time to the queen's cousin, Lettice Knollys. When Simier revealed the marriage to the queen, she flew into a rage, ordering Dudley to leave court.

A few days later, Alençon arrived in England for a formal visit. The forty-three-year-old Elizabeth behaved like a moonstruck girl when wooed by the young Frenchman. She spent hours alone with him and gave him expensive presents. She found him charming and completely believed his avowal of love. Furthermore, her pride had been stung by Dudley's marriage, and she was determined to gain revenge by marrying Alençon. In front of all the court she kissed him on the mouth and gave him a ring.

Another Disappointment

Alençon thought he had succeeded where so many others had failed, but he, too, was to be disappointed. Before any definite plans were made, Elizabeth reconsidered. Perhaps public opinion against the marriage had its effect. Perhaps her ingrained fear of marriage got the better of her. Or possibly it was her Gentlewomen and Maids of Honor, who were against the marriage, and, as historian William Camden later wrote, "by laying terrors before her, did so vex her mind

Elizabeth's Nicknames

Queen Elizabeth loved to give pet names and nicknames to the men she worked with and the men who courted her. William Cecil she called her "Spirit." Robert Dudley was her "Eyes," Sir Christopher Hatton her "Lids," and the swarthy, black-clad Sir Francis Walsingham her "Moor."

The duke of Alençon she nicknamed her "Frog," which gave rise to the song "Froggy Went a-'Courtin'." Alençon's envoy, Jean de Simier, she called "Monkey," and the earl of Essex, her last great favorite, was her "Wild Horse."

Some of these men took their nicknames to heart. Dudley would sign his letters with the symbol ◉◉. Hatton responded by signing his correspondence with a ⋀⋀.

with anguish, that she spent the night in doubteful care without sleepe, amongst her women which did nothing but weep."[43]

In any case, the next morning Alençon and Simier could tell that Elizabeth's attitude had changed. She was still affectionate but began to use the same delaying tactics she had employed with previous suitors. Although everyone now knew there would be no marriage, the formal negotiations dragged on until Alençon died five years later.

While there were no more serious suitors, there were plenty of favorites. Originally a member of the queen's bodyguard, Sir Christopher Hatton came to her attention because of his dancing ability and advanced rapidly. He became captain of the bodyguard in 1572 and vice chamberlain and a member of the Privy Council five years later.

Although Hatton's opponents sniffed and said he "came to court by the Galliard,"[44] a court dance, he was much more than just a man endowed with a pretty face and nimble feet. He developed into a true statesman and served sixteen years as Lord Chancellor of England, that is, the head of the House of Commons in Parliament. Unlike some who professed love for Elizabeth, Hatton seems to have meant it. He never married and served her faithfully until his death in 1591.

Raleigh

While Hatton caught the queen's eye while dancing, Sir Walter Raleigh, one of the most dashing figures at Elizabeth's court, is said to have used a very different approach. According to the story, never proved true, the queen was walking with her Maids of Honor in Greenwich Park in 1582 when she came to some boggy ground. Raleigh whipped off his expensive cloak and spread it on the mud for Elizabeth to walk upon. Supposedly

Sir Walter Raleigh offers his cloak to protect the queen's feet from the mud. Raleigh fell out of favor after his secret marriage was revealed.

she flashed him a dazzling smile in gratitude.

Whatever the truth in the story of the cloak, like Hatton, Raleigh rose rapidly. He was knighted in 1587 and two years later became captain of the queen's guard, growing rich from the monopolies she granted to him. Unlike Hatton, however, he did not bestow his devotion exclusively on Elizabeth. He secretly married in 1588, and the secret came out in 1592 when his wife gave birth to a son. The queen had both Raleigh and his wife thrown in prison. He managed to gain his release by paying a huge fine, but he never regained his place in Elizabeth's court.

Essex

Elizabeth's last great favorite, and one she loved more than any, except possibly Dudley, was Robert Devereaux, earl of Essex. But where her love for Dudley had been that of a young woman for a man her own age, her infatuation with Essex was that of an old woman for a vain young boy. Essex was the son of Robert Dudley's wife, Lettice Knollys, by her first marriage. He was sponsored at court by Dudley and found favor with Elizabeth, even though she had grown to hate his mother.

Essex's star rose about the same time Raleigh's was falling. The queen made him Master of Horse in 1587. Like Raleigh, he married in secret, but Elizabeth was so fond of him that she forgave him after only two weeks. Indeed, she could hardly bear to be parted from him. A contemporary

Elizabeth was infatuated with Robert Devereaux, the earl of Essex. She tolerated his many disrespectful acts until he committed treason, a crime she could not forgive.

writer said, "When she is abroad, no boddy neare here but my Lord of Essex; and at night my Lord is at cards, or one game or another with her, that he cometh not to his owne lodginge tyll birds sing in the morninge."[45]

Essex was so sure of himself that he acted toward Elizabeth in ways that no one else had ever dared. And, for the most part, he got away with it, although at one point she grumbled, "By God's death, it were fitting some one should take him down and teach him better manners, or there were no rule with him."[46]

And yet, she failed herself to take him down, although Essex gave her ample cause. Once, after an argument in front of the court, Essex defied all custom and turned his back on his queen who, infuriated, struck him a blow on the ear. Essex then compounded his error by laying his hand on the hilt of his sword as if to draw it.

The Fall of Essex

Finally, Essex went too far. Elizabeth had sent him to command troops in Ireland and had expressly forbidden him to return to England without her permission. He returned anyway and burst into her bedroom when she was without her makeup or wig. She received him graciously, but the next day he was placed under house arrest. Now even Essex realized he was in serious trouble. In desperation he tried to lead a rebellion, but it was poorly planned and failed utterly.

Insults were one thing, but treason was something Elizabeth could not and would not forgive. She later told the French ambassador that she had warned Essex to be "careful not to touch the scepter."[47] The earl was found guilty of treason and beheaded on February 25, 1601.

Cecil

There were men at Elizabeth's court, of course, who were neither suitors nor favorites, but members of her Privy Council to whom she trusted most of the running of the country. Chief among these was Sir William Cecil, who had been close to her during Mary's reign, and who Elizabeth had appointed as her secretary the day after Mary died. In so doing, she told him, "This judgment I have of you, that you will not be corrupted with any gift; and that you will be faithful to the state; and that without respect of my private will, you will give me that counsel that you think best."[48]

Cecil would follow these instructions, serving Elizabeth faithfully until his death in 1598. The job was not always easy. He had to put up with his mistress's many moods, and he knew them better than anyone else. He followed her instructions and told her when he thought she was wrong even though he knew his advice would unleash her anger. He weathered the storms philosophically, once writing, "Lord God be thanked, her blasts be not as the storms of other princes, though they be shrewd sometimes to those she loveth best."[49]

Elizabeth respected Cecil as perhaps she respected no other person. She once said that no ruler in Europe had a better servant than she had in her secretary. When he lay dying, worn out by years of hard work and sacrifice, she visited him each day, feeding him soup with her own hand. For months after he died she could not bear to hear his name mentioned at the Privy Council table without turning her head aside to weep.

Walsingham

She had no such affection for the other outstanding minister in her service, Sir

Sound Advice

Elizabeth I's most faithful councillor was William Cecil, Lord Burleigh. He served as her principal secretary for many years and afterward as Lord Treasurer. Late in life, in training his son Robert to take his place in the queen's service, he offered this advice, found in A Portrait of Elizabeth I, *edited by Roger Pringle.*

I do hold, and will always, this course in such matters as I differ in my opinion from her Majesty: as long as I may be allowed to give advice I will not change my opinion by affirming the contrary, for that were to offend God, to whom I am sworn first; but as a servant I will obey her Majesty's commandment and no wise contrary the same, presuming that she being God's chief minister here, it shall be God's will to have her commandments obeyed; after that I have performed my duty as a councilor, and shall in my heart wish her commandments to have such good success as I am sure she intendeth.

The queen relied heavily upon the counsel of William Cecil.

Francis Walsingham. A devout Puritan, he disapproved of most of what he considered the frivolities of court life. Nevertheless, that very religious zeal drove him to serve Elizabeth. "I wish God's glory and next the queen's safety"[50] was his motto. He knew that much of Catholic Europe would like to see her assassinated and made it his life's mission to see that she was protected. He did so by establishing a network of spies, both in England and throughout Europe, that allowed him knowledge of plots against her in time to snare all involved.

Elizabeth confers with government minister Sir Francis Walsingham. Although the queen did not care for Walsingham, she respected his zeal in protecting her throne.

Elizabeth respected Walsingham, but she did not like him. Possibly as a consequence, she did not make him wealthy, as she did Cecil, and when he died he was heavily in debt. True, the queen had given him several posts that carried incomes, but he spent most of his money paying his many spies. Elizabeth did, however, grant his last request, which was that he be buried quickly and without fanfare so that his creditors would not seize his body.

In dealing with all the men of her court—suitors, courtiers, councillors—Elizabeth took care to conceal her innermost thoughts and feelings. Dudley and Cecil knew her best but admitted that they could never predict her moods or actions. One court observer wrote that she "was by art and nature so blended, it was difficult to find her right humour at any time."[51] Through a combination of indecision, flirtation, blazing anger, and open affection, she was able to ensure that her court, as she told Dudley, had one mistress and no master.

All the Queen's Women

I f the men of Elizabeth's court found life with her majesty demanding, the women—those of the Privy Chamber, at least—found it difficult at best, impossible at worst. After all, they had to be with the queen day and night. They were subject not only to her public moods, but also to her private passions, which could range from praise and kisses to curses and blows. They endured it all, both for love of Elizabeth and love of the exciting life of her court.

The Gentlewomen who attended to the queen's physical needs were usually relatives or friends of long standing. The Maids of Honor, whose chief duty was companionship, were chosen for their family background, attractiveness, intelligence, and skills. Elizabeth expected them to be well educated and good conversationalists. They also were required to have talents such as dancing and singing, horseback riding, sewing, and cooking, preferably in the French style.

As a group, the Maids of Honor frequently provided a picturesque backdrop for the queen. They would dress in clothing styled to contrast with and set off whatever Elizabeth wore. They dressed attractively, but their garments were in no way supposed to rival those of the queen.

A Dress Too Fine

On at least one occasion, a Maid of Honor forgot this basic rule. Mary Howard, having caught the eye of the earl of Essex,

Advice to a New Maid of Honor

When Lady Bridget Manners received an appointment as a Maid of Honor in 1594, her family asked her granduncle, Sir Roger Manners, a court official, to give her some advice. He did so in a letter, this excerpt from which is found in Queen Elizabeth's Maids of Honour *by Violet Wilson.*

First and above all thinges that you forget not to use daly prayers to the Almightie God to endue you with his grace; then that you applie yourself hollye to the service of her majestie with all meekness love and bedizens [modesty]; wherein you must be diligent, secret and faythfull. To your elders and superiors, of reverent behaviour, to your equalles and fellow-servants syvill and courtesy; to your inferiors you must show all favour and gentleness. Generally that you be no medeler in the causes of others. That you use moch sylens, for that becometh maydes, especially of your calling. That your speech and indevars ever tend to the good of all and to the hurt of none. Thus in breve madam have you thes rules; which, if you have grace to follow you shall fynd the benefit, and your friends shall rejoice of your well doying.

tried to keep it by dressing extravagantly. One day she drew attention to herself by wearing a velvet dress decked with pearls, standing out from her comrades almost as much as did the queen, who decided to put her in her place.

One evening Elizabeth had the dress delivered to her from Lady Mary's wardrobe and put it on. Since she was much taller than her maid, the dress was too tight and the skirt and sleeves much too short. Thus attired, the queen marched into the room where the maids sat. Stopping before the frightened owner, she asked if she thought the dress ill fitting. The girl had to agree, whereupon the queen snapped, "Why then, if it become not me as being too short, I am minded that it should never become thee as being too fine; so it fitteth neither well."[52] The dress was never seen again.

Deception

Elizabeth sometimes found uses for her women other than companionship or ornamentation. When she was being courted by the Archduke Charles of Austria in 1559, she wanted to keep him interested—and thus keep Austria friendly toward England—but did not wish to commit herself to marriage. Instead, she told Lady Mary Sidney, Robert Dudley's sister, to tell Charles's ambassadors that their chances were excellent. Mary was supposed to say that if the queen seemed hesitant, it was because "as it is the custom of ladies here not to give their consent in such matters until they are teased into it."[53]

Weeks went by and Elizabeth still refused to give the ambassadors an answer. Finally, they pressed her, saying they had received assurances from someone close to her that she would marry the archduke. The queen blandly told them that whoever told them such a thing had done so without her permission. Mary Sidney was resentful at having been used as a pawn in the queen's game, but there was nothing she could do.

If the queen wanted to involve some of her women in matters of state, that was one thing. If they decided to involve themselves, that was quite another. Prince Eric of Sweden had been wooing the queen, and two of her Gentlewomen, Catherine Ashley and Dorothy Bradbelte, eager to see her married, wrote to him on their own, giving him their advice. Ashley had been Elizabeth's governess when she was a little girl, but it did not prevent her from feeling the queen's anger. The two women were placed under house arrest. Their confinement lasted only a month, but it doubtless sent a strong message to any others who might think about carrying on their own diplomatic correspondence.

Much the same thing occurred many years later when the earl of Essex had been arrested for treason. He had always been a favorite of Elizabeth's Gentlewomen and Maids of Honor, and some of them were

brave enough to try to plead his case with the queen. Her cousin, Lady Scrope, got down on her knees in mourning clothes on Essex's behalf, but Elizabeth was unmoved.

Mary Sidney's Tragedy

As with the men of the court, faithful service by women sometimes went unrewarded. In 1562 an epidemic of smallpox swept the court and the queen herself was not spared. Mary Sidney, the same woman through whom she had fed false information to the Austrian ambassador, remained by her bedside almost constantly. Like the queen, she contracted smallpox but, unlike Elizabeth, she was left terribly disfigured

Robert Devereaux, the earl of Essex, was executed for treason, despite the pleas of Elizabeth's Gentlewomen and Maids of Honor on his behalf.

by scars after the sores healed. Her husband, who had been away, said upon seeing her, "I left her a full fair lady—in mine eyes, at least, the fairest. And when I returned I found her as foul a lady as the smallpox could make her."[54]

Lady Sidney withdrew from court and went to her husband's home in the country. She lived, for the most part, behind closed shutters in dim rooms, receiving almost no visitors. In 1578, however, she accompanied her husband to the royal palace at Hampton Court. She found that, despite her condition, she and her husband had been assigned only one room, which also had to serve as a place for her husband to conduct meetings. She sent word to Elizabeth, trying to get larger quarters, but never received an answer.

The Way to the Queen

No matter how close they were to the queen, none of the women of the court held official administrative positions; their power lay in their proximity to their mistress. Since they were in her presence almost constantly, they grew used to her personality and could tell at a glance if the royal mood was fair or stormy. The men of the court, before they sought to ask something of Elizabeth, often consulted one of the women of the Privy Chamber to see which way the wind blew. When Robert Dudley was trying to win Elizabeth's hand in marriage, for example, he counted on Blanche Parry to tell him if the queen was in a receptive frame of mind.

When the women carried requests to the queen on someone's behalf, they expected to get some kind of gift in return. However, not all of them used their positions for gain. Many simply enjoyed the thrill of being at the center of events and having the most powerful men in England seek their help. It must, for example, have been satisfying for young Maid of Honor Elizabeth Stafford to be asked by the Archbishop of Canterbury, highest-ranking clergyman in the country, to "speak some good word"[55] to the queen.

The women of the court certainly would have needed money, since they found life there expensive. When Elizabeth Spencer, daughter of the wealthy Lord Mayor of London, married Lord Compton, she was determined to cut a fine figure at court. She wrote to her husband outlining what such a lifestyle would require. Included were a yearly allowance of £1,600, with an extra £600 for clothing; three horses; two gentlewomen; six or eight gentlemen; two coaches, with horses; two footmen; a gentleman-usher; £2,000 spending money; £6,000 for jewels; and £4,000 "to buy me a pearl chain." She ended by writing, "Now, seeing I have been and am so reasonable unto you, I pray you find all my servants, the men and women, their wages."[56]

A Lively Existence

Living at court may have been costly, but it was also very lively, especially for the

Two of the Queen's Gentlewomen appear in the group behind her. Although such women had no administrative authority, their proximity to Elizabeth led powerful men to consult them before approaching the queen.

a Privy Councillor and the queen's Vice Chamberlain. One night the maids, who included Knollys's daughter, were making so much noise that the grave Knollys stripped to his nightshirt and, according to an account of the time, "so with a payre of spectacles on his nose, and [a book on theology] in his hand, come marching in at the postern door of his own chamber, reading very gravely, full upon the faces of them. Now let the reader judge what a sadd spectacle a pittifull fright these poor creatures endur'd, for he faced them and often travest the roome in this posture about an hour."[57]

While the maids' life was lively, it was not always luxurious. When their mistress moved from palace to palace, living quarters sometimes changed for the worse. While the dormitory at Whitehall might be spacious, the one at Windsor was cramped and uncomfortable. Indeed, while at Windsor the maids requested "to have their chamber ceiled [a ceiling put in], and the partition that is of boards there to be made higher, for that the [other] servants look over."[58]

young Maids of Honor. They were among the great and powerful all day, with the queen at night and at bedtime in their dormitory, they chatted, gossiped, and played—sometimes to excess. At one point, the maids' dormitory was next to the room occupied by Sir Francis Knollys,

The Maids and Marriage

Despite discomforts, one reason that women—particularly young women—were eager to serve Elizabeth was that it was a way to meet, and perhaps marry, a rich nobleman. Marriage, however, was something of a dangerous subject to raise around Elizabeth. The queen, having herself resolved never to marry, was seldom eager for anyone else to do so, especially those close to her. The maids knew this well, and when Elizabeth asked them what they thought about marriage, wrote her godson Sir John Harrington, "the wise ones did well conceal their liking thereto."[59] When a Maid of Honor asked for permission to marry, Elizabeth might give her assent, but only after intense questioning, a display of temper and—in many cases—weeks or months of waiting.

Some daring women, either because they did not want the trouble of getting permission or they knew it would be refused, married secretly. When the queen found out—and she usually did—there was trouble. When Elizabeth discovered the marriage of Mary Shelton and James Scudamore, she "delt liberall both with bloes and yevell words."[60] Indeed, she grew so violent that in grabbing the girl's hand she broke a finger. To her credit, Elizabeth was ashamed of what she had done. She not only sanctioned the marriage, but also appointed the bride a Gentlewoman of the Bedchamber.

Bess Throckmorton, daughter of Sir Nicholas Throckmorton, England's longtime ambassador to France, was not as fortunate. Her husband of choice was Sir Walter Raleigh, one of the queen's fa-

The Maids of Honor disliked Windsor Castle (pictured) because their cramped rooms lacked privacy.

vorites. When the couple married sometime in late 1591, Bess was already pregnant. Amazingly, she was able to stay in Elizabeth's service until the final months before the child was born, when she left on some pretext.

After the birth of her baby in March, Lady Raleigh returned to court the next month as though nothing had happened. Rumors soon reached Elizabeth's ears, however, and in July both Raleigh and his wife were arrested and sent to the Tower of London. Raleigh was released after a few weeks, but the queen often dealt more harshly with the women involved in such marriages than with their husbands, and Bess remained imprisoned until December.

Similarly, Raleigh was able to regain his position at court—though he never had the same standing with the queen as before—but Elizabeth's mercy did not extend to his wife. Despite everything she did, or people tried to do on her behalf, she never gained what one of her former rivals called "that restitution in court which flattery had led her to expect."[61]

Catherine Grey

Those who married in secret played a much more dangerous game when Elizabeth's security on the throne was involved. One of her Maids of Honor was Lady Catherine Grey, a cousin of the queen and younger sister of Lady Jane Grey, who had been executed for treason. The fact that Catherine was one of Elizabeth's Maids of Honor likely was

Sir Walter Raleigh (pictured) and his wife were arrested and imprisoned after the jealous queen learned of their secret marriage.

due to the queen wanting to keep a close watch on the girl who, as a direct descendant of Henry VII, might have a claim, however slim, to the crown. However, the watch Elizabeth kept was not close enough. While on a visit to the home of Jane Seymour, her best friend among the maids, Catherine fell in love with Jane's brother Edward, the earl of Hertford.

The couple knew that, because of Catherine's kinship to Elizabeth, permission would be difficult to get. Hertford was afraid to approach the queen in person, so they asked Catherine's mother to write a letter to the queen on their

Jane Seymour (pictured) helped her brother Edward and Lady Catherine Grey to marry in secret. Their union incurred the queen's wrath.

Jane and a priest who had been hurriedly recruited, the two were married.

For a time the couple were able to keep their marriage secret, but after a few furtive encounters, Catherine found herself pregnant. To make matters worse, Elizabeth had ordered Hertford abroad. Catherine knew their secret would come out, and finally asked Lady St. Lo, one of the women of the bedchamber, for advice. This lady rebuked Catherine for burdening her with this news, but she did not tell the queen.

The Queen Is Told

Desperate, Catherine turned to the queen's greatest favorite, Robert Dudley. She entered his bedroom in the middle of the night, knelt by his bed, and confessed what had happened. Since Dudley's room, at the time, was next to Elizabeth's, he did all he could to get her out as quickly as possible, promising to tell the queen. He did so the next morning.

Elizabeth exploded with rage. Catherine was sent to the Tower of London, as was Lady St. Lo. So was Hertford, after being immediately recalled from duty. The baby—a boy—was born in September 1561. The Lieutenant of the Tower, in charge of the prisoners, took pity on the young couple and allowed them occasion-

behalf. Before the letter could be finished, however, Catherine's mother died. Lacking her help, the couple decided to wed without permission.

One day when the queen was out hunting, Catherine and Jane Seymour slipped out of Whitehall Palace, walked along the Thames River bank, and entered Hertford's house through the back door. There, in the presence of al visits. As a result, Catherine again became pregnant and a second son was born in 1562.

This was too much for Elizabeth. Hertford was fined the enormous sum of £15,000, the marriage declared invalid, and the two boys declared illegitimate. Her action in so doing was just as much out of political precaution as of revenge, since Catherine's sons, as male descendants of Henry VII, might possibly someday pose a threat to her rule. Hertford tried to show that the marriage had been lawful, but Jane Seymour had died by this time, and the priest— no one had thought to ask his name—

could not be found.

Shortly thereafter, when a plague was raging in London, Elizabeth allowed Hertford and his wife to leave the Tower, but to different destinations. When Catherine arrived at the home of her uncle, Lord John Grey, she said, "Alas, Uncle, what a life is this to me, thus to live in the Queen's displeasure. But for my Lord [Hertford] and my children I would I were buried."[62] Six years later she died at the age of twenty-nine.

Secret Affairs

If Elizabeth disapproved of marriage among members of her court, she disapproved of

---

The Perils of Honesty

Most of Queen Elizabeth's Maids of Honor knew better than to speak about their dreams of marriage in the presence of their mistress, who disliked the subject. One new maid, however—a Mistress Arundel, as related in Queen Elizabeth's Maids of Honour—*innocently told the queen that she thought much about marriage and wanted her father to give consent to the man she loved.*

"You seem Honestie, I' faith," the queen said. "I will sue for you to your father."

When the queen questioned the father, Sir Robert Arundel, she was angry to discover that he knew of no such love affair. Elizabeth convinced him to allow consent for any marriage to remain with her instead of him. When he had done so, she sent for the daughter and announced that her father had left everything in the queen's hands.

"Then I shall be happy, an' please your Grace," said Mistress Arundel unwarily.

"So thou shalt," snapped the queen, "but not to be a fool and marry. I have his consent given to me, and I vow thou shalt never get it into thy possession."

---

extramarital sex even more. History has left many examples, and that of Mary Fitton, one of the Maids of Honor, is typical. Shortly after coming to court at the age of seventeen, she began a love affair with the earl of Pembroke. To get out of the dormitory at night, she would remove her headwear, tuck her skirts under a long, white cloak, and march through the palace as if she were a man.

Eventually, Mary became pregnant, but Pembroke, instead of making her his countess, rejected any idea of marriage. Mary was placed under house arrest until the child was born, then banished to the country, where she had yet another illegitimate child by another lover.

Elizabeth, meanwhile, clapped Pembroke in prison. When he heard of Mary's subsequent conduct, he wrote verses to her, including the following:

Then this advice, fair creature, take from me,

Let none pluck fruit unless he plucks the tree,

For if with one, with thousands thou'lt turn whore,

Break ice in one place and it cracks the more.[63]

The perfect Maid of Honor, in Elizabeth's eyes, was Mary Radcliffe, who seemed to share her ideas on marriage. When a courtier wrote her flowery poems, she dismissed him, saying that "his wit was like custard, nothing good in it but the sop, and when that was eaten you might throw away the rest."[64] After one brief and unexciting courtship, she refused all other advances, serving her queen in determined spinsterhood for forty years.

Despite everything, the occasional discomfort and royal displeasure, to serve the queen could be rewarding in a number of ways, and there was no lack of candidates for positions among the women of Elizabeth's court. When Lady Leighton was considering retirement as a Gentlewoman of the Bedchamber in 1597, one courtier reported to another, "Here is already a whole dozen of ladies that would succeed her."[65]

The Court at Home

Queen Elizabeth I was not much of a builder of palaces. After all, palaces cost money. Fortunately for her, however, her father and grandfather had constructed or rebuilt many royal residences that were among the finest in Europe. They were so impressive that in 1559 an Austrian ambassador, in England seeking Elizabeth's hand in marriage for the Archduke Charles, wrote, "I have seen several very fine summer residences that belong to her . . . and I may say that there are none in the world so richly garnished. . . . Hence she is well worth the trouble."[66]

While certainly not comfortable by modern standards, the Tudor mansions that made up the royal residence were vast improvements over the immense stone castles of the previous centuries. Until the days of Elizabeth's grandfather, Henry VII, security, not comfort, had been the primary concern, so castles were designed with thick stone walls and tiny windows to keep out invaders. Unfortunately for the occupants, the walls and windows also kept out sunshine and fresh air.

Henry VII wanted no such castles in his kingdom, seeing them as potential fortresses in which a rebellious subject could take refuge. Stone castles designed for defense had to be licensed by the crown, and unlicensed castles were torn down. Anyway, massive stone castles had largely outlived their usefulness. The thick walls that might repel an army armed with bows and swords now could be battered down with the cannons that had been steadily improved in size and power.

Country Houses

As a result, large, graceful country houses began to replace castles. Bricks and timber replaced huge blocks of stone as building materials. Sheer walls pierced by narrow slits gave way to banks of windows. There were so many windows at one house built during Elizabeth's reign that people joked about "Hardwick Hall, more glass than wall."[67]

Instead of fortresses, the nobility lived in what one owner called a "romancy pleasant place."[68] "Romancy" they certainly could be. Pleasant they often were not. Perfume and incense could never mask the assortment of foul smells that permeated even the royal palaces. These odors were produced by hundreds of pounds of daily kitchen refuse and the large amount of animal and human waste, not to mention the animals and humans themselves. Hundreds of persons lived in cramped quarters. Even the grandest nobles bathed only infrequently and the servants bathed not at all. An

Hardwick Hall, built during Elizabeth's reign, was but one of her many country houses.

observer wrote that the air even in the queen's bedchamber was sour.

The fact that many of Elizabeth's principal palaces—Greenwich, Whitehall, and Hampton Court among them—were located on the banks of the Thames River was no help. Even though the river was by far the easiest way to travel, since roads were often rough and muddy, it was where the waste was thrown, not only from the palaces, but also from every town along its banks. To protect themselves from the stink of the river, Elizabeth and her courtiers held pomanders, containers holding perfume or sweet-smelling herbs, to their noses. Pomanders were also used on a daily basis in the palaces.

Water Supplies

Because of all that was dumped into it, the river was much too foul to be a source for drinking water for the palaces, so lead pipes had to be extended to nearby springs. These pipes brought water not only for drinking and washing, but also for the many fountains in which Elizabethans delighted. Getting water to the palaces was sometimes an impressive feat of engineering. The pipes to Hampton Court extended three miles—part of it under the Thames itself—and used 250 tons of lead.

It took plenty of water—indeed, plenty of everything—to supply the needs of the court. With more than a thousand people in residence, the amount of food needed was enormous. A visitor from

Spain during the reign of Queen Mary wrote, "The ordinary consumption of the Palace [Richmond] every day is from eighty to a hundred sheep, with a dozen fat oxen and a dozen and a half of calves, besides vast quantities of game, poultry, venison, wild boar and rabbits, whilst in beer they drink more in summer than the river would hold at Valladolid [a city in Spain]."[69] Consumption would have been every bit as large in Elizabeth's court. The English, in fact, had a reputation throughout Europe as prodigious eaters and drinkers.

Controlling the cost of such a vast amount of food proved impossible, since courtiers routinely disregarded restrictions put in place by the Lord Chamberlain. They ordered as much as they wanted of whatever they wanted from the royal kitchens and sometimes even raided the larders for food to send to their own homes. Even the Maids of Honor engaged in gluttony. In 1576, the budget for their meals was £495, but the actual expense was £680. The Gentlewomen of the Bedchamber were no better.

Too Many Cooks

One of the reasons that so much food vanished from the royal larders was that the higher-ranking members of the court had their own cooks. Also, it was hard to keep a watchful eye on the pantry when there were as many as eighteen kitchens, which was the case at Richmond. The same Spaniard that commented on the amount of food also wrote, "There is

Elizabethans were noted for their love of food and drink. Lavish banquets, like this one in the Hampton Court presence chamber, were hugely expensive.

such a hurly-burly in them [the kitchens] that each one is a veritable hell. So that notwithstanding the greatness of these palaces—and the smallest of the four we have been in has more rooms and better than the Alcazar [a palace] of Madrid—the crowds in them are so great as to be hardly contained."[70]

Yet, despite the lack of sanitation and crowded conditions, the court of Elizabeth was one of the showplaces of Europe. This was especially true when the queen wanted to impress foreign visitors. In 1601, for instance, the Italian duke of Bracciano and an ambassador from the emperor of Russia came at the same time and Elizabeth went all out to make theirs a memorable visit.

The four chambers the visitors were to occupy at Whitehall Palace were sumptuously furnished. Servants were busy "making clean the glass windows to give good light" and cooks were told to make sure that "the banquet be of better stuff, fit for men to eat and not of paper shows."[71] The queen ordered that a new play be written for the banquet, which was to be on the religious holiday of Epiphany, January 6. The playwright chosen for this task was William Shakespeare, and the work he produced for the occasion was *Twelfth Night*.

"A Marvelous Thing"

The foreign visitors were suitably impressed. The Italian duke wrote to his wife about the chief officers of the court "all dressed in white—as was the whole court that day—but with so much gold and jewels that it was a marvelous thing. . . . Nor do I believe that I shall ever see a Court which, for order, surpasses this one."[72]

The magnificence of Elizabeth's palaces extended to everyday furnishings. Expensive tapestries, one of them taken as a prize by King Henry V during the Hundred Years' War in the early 1400s, covered the walls. Satin and other expensive materials furnished upholstery for the furniture, the wooden portions of which were often covered with gold leaf. Even Elizabeth's close-stools, or portable toilets, were cases upholstered in satin and velvet.

For sheer grandeur, however, little surpassed the royal bedchamber. The bed itself, visitor Paul Hentzner wrote in 1598, was "ingeniously composed of woods of different colours, with quilts of

The Qualities of Servants

Running a large household in Elizabethan times required a small army of servants. Lord Willoughby de Eresby, one of Elizabeth's courtiers who left to set up his own household, drew up a lengthy list of rules for his servants to follow, concluding with this passage, found in Queen Elizabeth's Maids of Honour *by Violet Wilson.*

I do wish and heartily desire that all my servants should be of godly virtuous and honest conversation, refraining from vicious living, unseemly talk, excessive drinking, seditious language, mocking, scoffing, or misnaming, and that by abstaining from variance, dissensions, debates, frays, sowing of discord, malice, envy and hatred, they shall live and continue in all friendly affection together, as it becometh the body of one family, to love the one the other; and towards all strangers to be of honest and courteous entertainment. By which doings, God will sooner bless my proceedings.

silk velvet, gold, silver, and embroidery."[73] Another bed was made of walnut and covered with carvings of mythological beasts. Elizabeth so liked this particular bed that it would be dismantled and moved when she changed residences.

Elizabeth changed residences often. She had a restless nature and would frequently pace to and fro while talking to her councillors. She also enjoyed seeing other places and other faces and—more important—giving more people an opportunity to see her. Her travels took her from palace to palace and, in the summer, on extended tours, or "progresses," throughout the kingdom.

There was also an extremely practical reason for the frequent change of abode. The crowded and unsanitary conditions, after a few months, rendered the palaces almost uninhabitable. Therefore, after the queen moved on—taking along many of the rich furnishings—a palace was "sweetened." Servants swarmed over the building and grounds—airing rooms, scrubbing floors, cleaning out stables, making repairs—to prepare for the time months and sometimes years distant when the court would return.

Elizabeth's Palaces

There were many royal palaces, far too many for Elizabeth to visit every year. Among those she lived in less frequently than others were Woodstock, Hatfield, Oatlands, Newhall, and Windsor. Oatlands, southwest of London, was a favorite spot for hunting, and Newhall was to the north-east, about halfway between London and the North Sea port of Harwich. Windsor, being for the most part the old-style stone castle, held little attraction for the queen, but she sometimes went there in times of national emergency, such as when a rebellion or invasion was threatened.

Elizabeth had emotional—and very different—attachments to both Woodstock and Hatfield. Woodstock, just north of Oxford, had been a royal hunting lodge since the days of King Henry II in the 1100s. Elizabeth had been imprisoned there in 1554 when she was suspected of involvement in an uprising known as Wyatt's Rebellion. Even so, she paid several visits there.

Elizabeth had purchased Hatfield in 1550 when she was only sixteen years old. She spent most of the years up to Queen Mary's death there and always had a deep affection for the house and surrounding countryside.

Although she visited these palaces on occasion, she lived primarily at five—Greenwich, Whitehall, Richmond, Hampton Court, and Nonsuch. She had been born at Greenwich and had spent most of her childhood there. It was located east of London on the Thames estuary, and the sea breezes made it an attractive place to spend the spring and early summer months.

Greenwich

Greenwich had been a royal residence for more than a century but had been great-

From her bedroom window at Greenwich Palace (pictured), the queen waved merrily to sailors of the Royal Navy as their ships passed by on the Thames.

ly expanded and improved by Henry VIII, whose favorite home it was. Elizabeth would travel there on a barge rowed by twenty uniformed oarsmen, sitting in a cabin hung with gold and velvet cloth, the floor covered with flowers as a means of masking the smell of the river.

The barge would dock at a long brick waterfront designed to look like a fortress. Between the dock and palace was a large open area used for jousting or military displays. Elizabeth's private quarters faced the river, and one of her favorite pastimes was to sit in an open window, waving to the sailors of her navy as they sailed by while the ships' cannon boomed a salute.

Behind the palace rose a hill surmounted by an ancient tower built by Greenwich's original owner, the duke of Gloucester, during the Wars of the Roses. From the top there was a splendid view of the palace and river below and, far to the west, the church steeples of London. On the first day of May in the early years of her reign, Elizabeth and her courtiers who were able would climb the hill and "walk into the sweet meadows and green woods, there to rejoice [their] spirits with the beauty and savour of sweet flowers and with the harmony of birds, praising God after their kind."[74]

Whitehall

Upriver from Greenwich, near the center of government in Westminster, was Whitehall Palace. For centuries it had been known as York House and was the London home of the archbishop of York. It had been confiscated by Henry VIII, who had "brought it, by great expense, unto its present princely form."[75]

Just how princely Whitehall appeared was a matter of opinion. A German visitor, Lupold von Wedel, wrote in 1585 about "glorious Whitehall, a regal mansion . . . beautiful and large, adorned with many fair galleries."[76] However, an observer in the next century, Samuel de Sorbiére, called the palace "nothing but a heap of houses, erected at divers times and of different models."[77]

Most critics shared de Sorbiére's opinion. Indeed, Whitehall was a clutter of buildings linked by passageways and consisted of about two thousand rooms spread over twenty-three acres. To make matters worse, a major thoroughfare, King Street, split the palace in half, and people went from one side to the other through two arched gateways.

The interior of Whitehall was another matter. Even von Wedel, who admitted that some of Elizabeth's palaces were more attractive from the outside, added that they were "but inwardly not equal to this one."[78] The decorations were just as opulent as at the other palaces, and indeed some of them were the same ones moved from place to place, but Whitehall

Most observers considered Whitehall Palace unattractive. It was comprised of many buildings spread across twenty-three acres.

had something the others lacked—some of the finest art in Europe.

Most striking was an exquisite mural by the Swiss expatriate Hans Holbein the Younger, showing the entire royal family of Henry VIII and which occupied a whole wall of the Privy Chamber. The original would be lost when most of Whitehall was destroyed by fire in 1698, but Holbein had also rendered the family portrait on canvas. Centuries later, art critic Roger Fry would write that it has "all the grandeur of style, all the lucidity and ease or arrangement of the greatest monumental design of Italy."[79]

Whitehall was the scene of Elizabeth's lone venture into building. In 1581, when a delegation from France came to try to complete plans for the marriage of Elizabeth and the duke of Alençon, the queen had a new banqueting hall constructed for the event. She borrowed a page from her father's history by deciding to build what was really an elaborate tent.

The hall was 332 feet around and had 292 windows. The walls were made of canvas, but were painted to look like stone. On the ceiling, one of the French visitors reported, "was wrought most cunninglie upon canvas, works of ivie and hollie; with pendants made of wicker rods . . . all manner of strange flowers garnished with spangles of gold . . . with all manner of strange fruits, as pomegranates, orenges, pompions, cucumbers, grapes, carrets, with such other like, spangled with gold and most richlie hanged."[80]

The whole structure was held up by thirty wooden pillars forty feet high. It took three hundred workmen twenty days to construct the banqueting hall in time for the French visit. Although intended to be taken down soon after its initial use, the banqueting hall proved so popular that it was kept in good repair until it was finally torn down in 1607, four years after Elizabeth's death.

Richmond

A few miles up the river to the east of Whitehall, out of London and into the countryside, was Richmond Palace. Begun by Henry VII in 1498, it was the largest of the royal residences. Richmond had the reputation of being exceptionally comfortable, which is perhaps why the queen favored it in the winter. The great hall, for instance, had a huge open fireplace in the center, the smoke escaping through the ceiling by means of a large vent and pipe.

To the south, where the Thames loops to the west, lay Hampton Court. It was leased in 1514 by Cardinal Thomas Wolsey, at the time Henry VIII's Lord Chancellor. Wolsey set out to make it the finest palace in Europe and did such a good job that Henry grew jealous. To gain favor with the king, Wolsey gave Hampton Court to him.

The Paradise Chamber

The highlight of Hampton Court, to visitors, was the Paradise Chamber, a throne room in which Elizabeth liked to receive

Royal Tourist Attraction

When the queen was not in residence, her palaces were open to tourists . . . for a fee. A German visitor to Hampton Court, Thomas Platter, wrote this in 1599:

First we were shown . . . into a large and very long gallery hung all round with old woven tapestries. This led us to the dining or banqueting Hall, from which we entered the Church or Chapel containing a most excellent fine organ on which I played a while, then we inspected the gallery or loft from which the Queen listens to the sermon. On our descent and exit from the Church, the gardener presented himself, and after we had offered a gratuity [fee] to our first guide, the gardener conducted us into the Royal pleasure garden.

Another visitor, Justus Zinzerling, was upset at having to pay three times to complete the tour. He complained especially about the keeper of the Paradise Chamber, thought by many to be the most beautiful and most elegant in the kingdom. He wrote that "the keeper of this room is so sordid that you must bargain beforehand about his fee; yet from his dress he appears to be a grand gentleman."

The quotations are found in Palaces and Progresses of Elizabeth I *by Ian Dunlop.*

Like Elizabeth's other palaces, the doors of Hampton Court were open to visitors when the queen was not in residence.

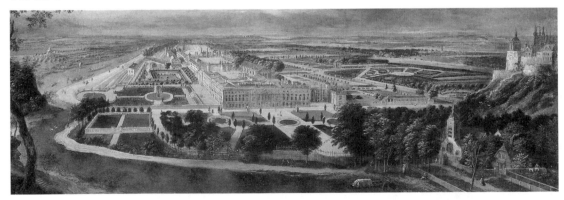

the most important foreign visitors. One such visitor called the Paradise Chamber "the most magnificent and most splendid room in the whole mansion, perhaps even in the whole realm."[81] The throne itself was upholstered in brown velvet decorated with gold embroidery, pearls, and three huge diamonds. Above was a canopy showing the royal arms of England in gold, surrounded by the emblem of the knightly Order of the Garter done in pearls and diamonds. Those who saw Elizabeth enthroned in this setting could not help but be impressed, which is doubtless what the queen had in mind.

Hampton Court would prove to be the only Tudor royal palace to survive to modern times intact. The others would fall into ruin like Richmond, be destroyed by fire like Whitehall, or be completely rebuilt in a newer style in later years as at Greenwich.

Nonsuch, located on a plain a few miles southeast of Hampton Court, was begun by Henry VIII in 1538 and so named because the king vowed that when it was finished there would be none such like it. Two great five-story towers, each level more heavily decorated than the next, dominated

the exterior. A gallery between them connected the king's and queen's apartments.

The inner courtyard drew praise from many visitors. Dr. Anthony Watson, a local clergyman, wrote, "When you have greeted its threshold and seen with eyes dazzled the shining luster of the stone, glittering with purest gold, it is not surprising if it should hold you senseless."[82] What Dr. Watson took for marble was actually white stucco. The huge central fountain surmounted by a white horse, however, was imported Italian marble. From such descriptions it is easy to see why Elizabeth often visited

Royal Residences and Points of Interest

Hardwick Hall
Kenilworth Castle
Burleigh House
Woodstock Palace
Newhall Palace
ENGLAND
Greenwich Palace
LONDON
Outlands Palace

In London:
The Globe
Hampton Court Palace
Nonsuch Palace
Richmond Palace
Tower of London
Westminster Abbey
Whitehall Palace
Windsor Castle

The knot gardens at Hampton Court. These intricately designed landscapes were much prized in the Elizabethan era.

Nonsuch, "which of all places she likes best."[83]

Nonsuch suffered perhaps the saddest fate of any of Elizabeth's palaces. In 1670, sixty-seven years after the queen died there, Nonsuch was given by King Charles II to a former mistress, Countess Castlemaine. In 1682 the countess, a notorious gambler, was so heavily in debt that she had the castle demolished, selling off all the materials and furnishings. The demolition was so complete that it would not be until 1959 that archaeologists would be able to ascertain where the palace had stood.

Elizabethan Gardens

The areas surrounding the royal palaces were just as important to the queen and her court as the interiors. The English in Elizabeth's time were great lovers of gardens, both the very formal, geometrically planned sort and the more unplanned park areas. The formal gardens were laid out in squares, or "knots," in which bushes and flowers were planted in complex geometrical patterns.

Another distinctive feature was the use of topiary, hedges sculpted into shapes of animals. A German visitor left a description of "all manner of shapes, men and women, half men and half horse, sirens, serving-maids with baskets . . . all round made from dry twigs bound together and the aforesaid evergreen quickset shrubs, or entirely of rosemary, all true to life . . . and arranged picture-wise that their equal would be hard to find."[84]

Statues were an important part of Elizabethan gardens, as were fountains and sundials. One sundial at Whitehall illustrated the Elizabethan love of practical jokes. It was said to show time in thirty different ways, but when a person paused to observe it, someone out of sight nearby could turn a valve, releasing jets of water from a hidden outlet to drench the unwary visitor.

Elizabeth and her courtiers were also fond of natural surroundings and would plant what they called wildernesses (as opposed to carefully tended parks). Dr. Watson wrote that at the wilderness at Nonsuch, "many people sit down and, dressed in the gayest of clothes, converse on various topics, listen to the calls of the animals and the song of the birds."[85]

Elizabeth's palaces, dotting the landscape around London, were the showpieces of England. The English author Daniel Defoe, writing in the following century, compared them to "jewels . . . in a rich coronet . . . at a distance they are all nature, near hand all art; but both in the extremest beauty."[86] And yet, life in Elizabeth's court could be demanding, both in terms of expense and in dealing with the queen's mercurial personality. It was no wonder that one courtier, even while extolling the beauty of the court, wrote, "Blessed are they that can be away and live contented."[87]

The Court on the Move

Queen Elizabeth I had a genuine desire to be among her people. She felt a real affection for her subjects and took very seriously her coronation vows to look after their welfare. She combined this attitude with a keen sense of politics. "She would show herself abroad at public spectacles, even against her own liking," wrote one observer, "to no other end but that the people might better perceive her ability of body and good disposition."[88] The strategy worked. The English had hardly known the aloof Henry VII, had been in awe of Henry VIII, and hated Mary, but they adored Elizabeth.

This desire to show herself to her people, combined with her restless per-

sonality, was so intense that moving from palace to palace was not enough. In addition, she spent much of the summer traveling throughout the kingdom on progresses, the court moving with her. While these journeys were memorable for the common folk who got to see their queen, they took their toll on the courtiers and were very much a mixed blessing for those who played host to the queen. A visit from Elizabeth was an honor, but a very expensive one.

Being queen meant never having to ask for permission to pay a visit or wait to be invited. As courtier William Harrison wrote, "Every nobleman's house is her palace, where she continueth during pleasure and till she return again to some of her own."[89] Some tried their best to avoid having Elizabeth as a guest. Some pleaded that their houses were too small or too uncomfortable. That made no difference to the queen, who was sure to get the best quarters anyway. The bishop of Winchester found that even claiming that plague was in a nearby village failed to dissuade her from visiting him.

Close to London

About the only sure means of escaping a royal visit was distance. Most of Elizabeth's twenty-three progresses took place within 50 miles of London, and the farthest she ever went was Worcester 130 miles away. The journeys usually began in July, "it being very unhealthy here [in London] this time of year,"[90] and lasted into September or, in rare cases, October. The number of places she visited ranged from six to twenty. The average visit lasted only two days but could be run on for more than a week.

The queen's hosts, whether reluctant or eager, usually found out about an upcoming visit from the royal Harbingers. These messengers announced their mistress's intentions, inspected the house and surrounding area, then rode on to the

Planning the Route

Planning an itinerary for the queen's progresses was sometimes an uncertain affair. In 1591 her Lord Chamberlain, Lord Hundson, wrote for help to Sir William Moore at Petworth. This excerpt is found in A Portrait of Elizabeth I, *edited by Roger Pringle.*

I have thought good to let you understand that her Majesty is resolved to make a Progress this year as far as Portsmouth, and to begin the same the 22 or 23 of this month, and to come to your house. She is very desirous to go to Petworth and Cowdray, if it be possible; but none of us all can set her down any where to lie at between your house and Cowdray. And therefore I am to require you that you will set this bearer [of the message] some way for her to pass, and that you will let some one of your own men who is best acquainted with that way, to be his guide, that he may see whether they be fit for her Majesty or no. And whether it will be best going from your house to Cowdray. And if you can set her down [at] any place between your house and Cowdray that may serve her for one night, you shall do her a great pleasure, and she will take it very thankfully at your hands.

next stop on the projected itinerary. Soon after came the Purveyors, members of the household charged with arranging for the purchase of supplies for the court. The supply requirements were enormous and one would have thought that local merchants would welcome the business, but this was not the case: Supplies were bought at prices set by the queen's officers, who knew well Elizabeth's thrifty nature and therefore paid as little as they could get away with.

News of the queen's upcoming visit would set off a frenzy of activity. Not only did the house need to be thoroughly cleaned, but lavish decorations were planned and extra supplies bought. The Purveyors never bought enough, and the hosts were eager to make sure there was food and drink in abundance.

Sometimes, when Elizabeth stayed in several houses in the same area, these supplies were hard to come by. Lord Buckhurst complained that he was "fain [forced] to send to Flanders [in the Netherlands] to supply him, the others having drawn the country dry."[91] There was a scramble, not only for basic necessities, but also luxuries. Before the queen's arrival at Cambridge University, for example, "all the velvets and silks were taken up that might be laid hands on and bought for money."[92]

No Certainty

Even when everything was almost ready, however, the hosts could not be sure if the queen would come exactly when planned. Sir Nicholas Bacon, whose house was supposed to be visited, wrote to William Cecil, at whose house she was staying, confessed to "knowing no certainty of the time of her coming nor of her abode," and urged Cecil to see that "this bearer my servant might understand what you know therein."[93]

Transporting Elizabeth and the court to the places she visited was just as difficult as preparing for the visit. There was seldom a convenient river, and the party was too large for river travel in any case. So, the procession had to go overland on rough, often muddy roads. Even in the next century, writer Daniel Defoe would report of a noble lady whose coach had to be drawn, not by horses, but by six oxen, which were much stronger.

While the entire court did not accompany Elizabeth on these travels, the number was still impressive—up to 350 people, not including servants. Observer Jacob Rathgeb wrote that when the queen set out, "there commonly follow more than three hundred carts laden with bag and baggage."[94] William Harrison wrote that the number was closer to four hundred and that the total procession required twenty-four hundred horses.

Early in her reign, Elizabeth would have ridden one of these horses, which were by far the most comfortable method of transportation. As she grew older, however, she was conveyed in something new to England—the coach. Coaches were introduced to the country in 1564 by a Dutchman, William Boonen, who

The queen slept in this sumptuous bedchamber when she visited William Cecil at his home, Burleigh House. Elizabeth's demands often tried the patience of her hosts.

became the queen's coachman. When the queen appeared in a coach upholstered in red leather with silver nails, all noble ladies wanted something similar and eventually "divers great ladies, with as great jealousy of the Queen's displeasure made them coaches, and rid them up and downe the countries to the great admiration of all beholders."[95]

Slow Going

Such a vast amount of people and provisions could not travel swiftly, especially since supplies were transported in wagons instead of on packhorses. Indeed, the cavalcade was lucky to cover three miles each hour. Harrison thought that, in addition to being slower, wagons lacked dignity. He complained that using them "causeth our princes in their progresses to show far less than those of the kings of other nations."[96]

Those people receiving Elizabeth as a guest went to great pains to outdo one another in the lavishness of their welcome. She could count on hearing one, and usually many more, elaborate orations extolling her beauty, wisdom, majesty, and any other virtue that came to mind. At Cowdray, the home of Lord Montague, a gatekeeper turned orator hailed her as "the wisest, fairest and most fortunate of all creatures. . . . O Miracle of Time! Nature's Glory! Fortune's Empress! The World's Wonder!"[97]

The queen never seemed to tire of hearing such pompous stuff, which usually was delivered by the local schoolmaster or clergyman. When visiting the city of Norwich in 1578, she listened attentively to a long and boring speech and then told the astounded speaker, "It is the best that ever I heard, and you shall have my hand [to kiss]."[98]

Probably no welcome equaled that which the queen received at the ancient castle of Kenilworth, home of Robert Dudley, which she visited in 1575. She was still seven miles from the castle when Dudley gave her a banquet in a tent specially built for the event and so large that it required seven carts to carry it.

As she approached the castle gatehouse, trumpeters on the walls sounded out a welcome. These trumpeters, however, were gigantic pasteboard figures behind which the real musicians stood. As she passed by the wide, deep moat in front of the castle, toward her floated an artificial island on which was someone dressed as the Lady of the Lake, a figure from the legends of King Arthur, who spoke her welcome. At last, as the queen entered the palace, there was "so great a peal of guns [that] the noise and flame were seen and heard twenty miles off,"[99] and the clock on the central tower was stopped so that time would stand still during her visit.

In 1575 Elizabeth visited Robert Dudley at his home, Kenilworth Castle (pictured). Dudley arranged a lavish display of pomp and ceremony in her honor.

Rush to Quarters

When the official welcome was at last over, it was time for everyone to find and settle into their living quarters—no easy task. There were never enough good rooms for all, and squabbles were sure to break out over who got them. Once when Sir Walter Raleigh moved into rooms designated for Sir Christopher Hatton, the two almost fought a duel. Sometimes the house simply was not large enough to accommodate everyone and tents had to do, much to the dismay of those who had to reside in them. When aging Sir Henry Lee, the queen's official champion for many years, saw a tent in which he was to reside, he announced that he had endured enough discomfort from progresses and retired from court the same year.

While most of the court disliked progresses, they dared not say so to the queen. Instead, they pretended to enjoy them as much as Elizabeth did. "Theye that shall attend the queens majestie in the progress shall swer from the hyest to the lowest to find solft wayes," the earl of Arundel wrote, "how hard soever they fynde theyr lodging & fare."[100]

Elizabeth enjoyed the progresses immensely, and for good reason. Her hosts went to extraordinary lengths and spared no expense to make her comfortable and keep her entertained. Her every suggestion was a command—or at least it was taken as such. Visiting Thomas Gresham in 1576, she remarked that a large courtyard would look better if divided by a wall. When she awoke the next morning, the wall was there, built swiftly and silently during the night by dozens of masons.

No Lake, No Problem

In 1591 Elizabeth visited Elvetham, home of one of her favorite former Maids of Honor, Frances Howard, wife of the earl of Hertford, the same man who many years before had incurred the queen's wrath by marrying Catherine Grey. Frances had been in court at the time of the famous progress to Kenilworth and knew how impressed Elizabeth had been with the floating island. She was determined to have an island, too, but Elvetham had no moat. To make one, three hundred workers dug night and day until they had a huge hole into which a nearby stream could be diverted.

This lake had not one island, but three. They did not float, but on one a small fort had been built, on the second a replica of a sailing ship, and on the third shrubs shaped to form a giant snail, symbolic of the monster of Catholic Spain. Taken together, the three islands were meant to commemorate the great naval battle four years earlier in which the English fleet had defeated the Spanish Armada.

Another imaginative host, Francis Carew, knew of Elizabeth's fondness for cherries, but her visit was planned for a time long after spring, when the fruit ordinarily ripened. To outwit nature,

Carew covered his cherry trees with a tent and kept the canvas soaked with cold water, creating wintry temperatures inside. Shortly before the queen's visit, he removed the tents and a few warm, sunny days produced fresh, ripe cherries for the queen's table.

Guest or not, Elizabeth rarely failed to speak her mind when something was not to her liking. Her comments could be blunt, but her hosts took them seriously. For example, when she visited Nicholas Bacon at Gorhambury she remarked, "My Lord Keeper, what a little house you have gotten."[101] Bacon took care to expand his house before time for the next visitation came.

Most people who anticipated a progress took pains to increase the size of their houses to accommodate, as much as was possible, the onslaught of guests. Cecil's great house, Theobalds, was the site of twelve visits during the reign, and Cecil was constantly making improvements. He did so with a good will for the sake of Elizabeth "whom to please I never would omit to strain myself to more charges than building it."[102]

Costly Visits

Hosting the queen, however, was a financial strain. The cost for food necessary to supplement what the royal Purveyors bought was enormous, to say nothing of the amount spent on entertainment. At Lord Montague's residence at Cowdray, the menu for a single meal was three oxen and 140 geese, and that was for a

While visiting Nicholas Bacon (pictured), Elizabeth bluntly remarked on the small size of his home. Bacon saw to it that the house was enlarged before her next visit.

breakfast. Nicholas Bacon spent £377, the equivalent of about $56,500 in modern terms, on food for a four-day visit.

The total bill for a host could run as high as £2,000 ($350,000), which Thomas Egerton paid in 1602. That, however, was at the end of the reign when prices had inflated and after decades of people trying to outspend one another. Most of the totals were far less, Cecil's £1,078 ($165,000) in 1591 being one of the more expensive. Compared to these, Nicholas Bacon got off relatively cheaply at £577 ($86,500).

These figures, however, did not include the gifts to the queen that were a traditional part of the progress. Sometimes the gift was in the form of money, which was certainly welcome to the frugal Elizabeth. On leaving Norwich she was handed a silver cup. She looked under the lid, saw it was filled with gold pieces, and told the crowd that "princes have no need of money,"[103] that the hearts of her people were gifts enough. Nevertheless, she quickly handed the cup to a footman, cautioning him, "Look to it; there is a hundred pound!"[104]

On other occasions, gifts took the form of rich gowns, jewelry, or plates of silver and gold. Elizabeth had high standards, however, and the gifts were expected to match the wealth of the giver. Evidently, whatever she was given by Lord Puckering was considered inadequate. A courtier accompanying the queen later wrote that she took from him, in addition, "a salt [cellar], a spoon, and a fork, of fair agate."[105]

Taking Leave

At the end of her visits her hosts proclaimed themselves heartbroken that she

Elizabeth traveled with a large retinue, and her hosts were expected to provide accommodations for this multitude of guests.

would leave. When she left Elvetham, she passed women costumed as the three mythological Graces and as hours of the day. Earlier, they had welcomed her with glad songs. Now, they wept, a contemporary account said, "all of them on every side wringing their hands, and shewing signe of sorrow for her departure" while a poet exclaimed,

> See where those Graces, & those Howrs of heav'n
>
> Which at thy coming sung triumphal songs,
>
> And smoothed the way, and strewd it with sweet flowrs,
>
> Now, if they durst, would stop it with green bowes,
>
> Least by thine absence the yeeres pride decay:
>
> For how can sommer stay, when Sunne departs?[106]

All expressions of woe to the contrary, Elizabeth's hosts were probably happy and relieved when, at last, her vast caravan had disappeared in the distance.

Most of the nobles who played host to Elizabeth on her progresses spent money with the hope of being granted some great favor in return. Certainly the earl of Hertford had reason to hope. When Elizabeth left Elvetham, she told him that "his entertainment was so honorable, as hereafter hee should finde the rewarde thereof in her especiall favor."[107] There were limits, however, to such a reward, as Hertford found when he subsequently sought to have his sons by the late Catherine Grey declared legitimate. Not only did the queen deny his request, but it cost him another stay in the Tower of London and another £15,000.

Such were the famous progresses of Queen Elizabeth I. The modern notion that she forced herself on her nobles in order to save money was not true. Indeed, each progress cost her about £1,000 above what she would have spent by staying at one of her own palaces. The purpose of the progresses, then, was not to save money, but for her to see her country and be seen by her subjects. The common people who lined the roads to get a glimpse of her probably told the story decades later to their grandchildren when Good Queen Bess went by in her coach, wrote nineteenth-century historian John Nichols, "like a goddess such as painters are wont to depict."[108]

Chapter 7

The Court at Play

Even though they might have titles—groom, keeper, master of this, mistress of that—suggesting otherwise, few of Elizabeth's courtiers actually had any real work to do. The nobles might have the titles, but servants performed the labor. Daily life at court therefore consisted of an endless pursuit of amusements and other diversions to keep tedium at bay.

At night there were banquets, accompanied by music and other entertainment, with dancing afterward. Courtiers also might be treated to a play or a ballet. They gambled at cards and other games or had their fortunes told.

Hunting and falconry were favorite daytime diversions for both men and women, and there frequently was jousting for the men. In bad weather, men might practice fencing and women would do needlework.

Music played an important part in the life of the court. Indeed, England of Elizabeth's time had a reputation among other European countries as the most musical of civilized nations. A small orchestra usually accompanied banquets from a small gallery or balcony above the hall and would be joined by other musicians to play afterward, either for dancing or in a concert.

The accomplished courtier was expected not only to listen to and appreciate music, but also to play an instrument as well, or at least to sing. The queen loved music and was said to be an excellent player on the virginal, a small harpsichord, and her instrument at Hampton Court had strings of silver and gold. The lute, a guitarlike instrument, was also popular with courtiers.

The Madrigal

For those who could not play musical instruments, there was always singing, and the madrigal was the favorite type of nonreligious music sung at court. It had originated in Italy but in England took on a much livelier, more rhythmic form. It featured multiple "voices," or melodies weaving in and out of one another.

Madrigals were written to be sung, but music for dancing was just as important, perhaps even more so, in Elizabeth's court. The queen was a highly skilled dancer and very proud of that skill. Even when she was too old for the faster dances, she enjoyed watching them. Late in the reign a French diplomat wrote,

> She takes great pleasure in dancing and music, in her youth she danced very well, and composed measures and music and had played them herself and danced them. She takes such pleasure in it that when her Maids dance she follows the cadence with her head, hand and foot. She rebukes them if they do not dance to her liking and without doubt she is a mistress of the art, having learnt in the Italian manner to dance very high.[109]

She once asked the ambassador from Scotland, Sir James Melville, who was the better dancer, herself or Mary, Queen of Scots. She was delighted when Melville said that Mary "danced not so high, and disposedly as she did."[110]

The Volta

Elizabeth was full of nervous energy, and dancing was one way in which she released it—a far better way, in her courtiers' eyes, than her occasional outbursts of temper. Indeed, the queen often began her day by dancing a galliard, a sprightly French dance, or two before breakfast. Her favorite, however, was the volta, a furious Italian two-step in which the man grasped his partner around the hips, lifted her off the floor, and whirled her around.

One enthusiastic dancer of the time wrote of the volta,

> Yet is there one the most delightful kind,
>
> A lofty jumping or a leaping round,
>
> Where arm in arm two dancers are entwin'd,
>
> And whirl themselves with strict embracements bound.[111]

Moralists decried the volta as lewd. Doctors worried that it was so violent that it might cause miscarriages in pregnant women. Elizabeth and her court, however, loved it.

The queen continued to dance until the final year of her life. On April 8, 1602,

King Henry VIII and Anne Boleyn (far left) passed on their flair for dancing to their daughter. Elizabeth particularly enjoyed dancing the volta, although moralists criticized the vigorous two-step as lewd.

sophisticated audiences of Elizabeth's court wanted plays of higher quality. This demand, in turn, motivated the writing of some of the greatest works in the English language, most notably those by Christopher Marlowe and William Shakespeare.

The queen's sponsorship not only fueled creativity among playwrights but also perhaps saved drama from being snuffed out. The Puritans, increasingly numerous and powerful in England, despised the theater as ungodly, but could not eliminate it so long as their monarch viewed it, as she put it, "as well for the recreation of our loving subjects as for our solace and pleasure."[113]

eleven months before her death, she danced a galliard with a French duke to open a ball. The French ambassador wrote admiringly that she danced "with a disposition admirable for her age."[112]

Elizabethan Drama

The court also loved plays, no one more than the queen. Her enthusiasm for plays led to the flowering of English drama. Roving bands of actors had been popular in England for many years, but the plays themselves had been little more than melodramas or slapstick comedy. The more

It was during Elizabeth's reign that the first permanent theaters were built, not in London, but on the south bank of the Thames in Southwark. Among them was the famous Globe, where many of Shakespeare's works were first performed. The queen, however, would not have attended a performance there—virtually no lady of quality did. Instead, the theater companies would have come to the palace, as they did when *Twelfth Night* made its debut at Hampton Court.

Although they could be complex and subtle, there was little about Elizabethan plays that could be called dainty or refined. The comedies, which the queen loved best, were bawdy. Likewise, audiences expected the tragedies and historical dramas to be full of action that was as lifelike as possible. Violent death was an integral part of these plays and to make it seem real, the Master of the Revels, who arranged the performances and was responsible for helping find necessary props, had to come up with "legs and arms of men, well and lively wrought, were to be let fall in numbers on the ground as bloody as might be."[114]

In addition to drama, poetry flourished in Elizabeth's court, much of it directed at her. One of the hallmarks of the accomplished courtier was the ability to write verse, and some of the most outstanding poets of the age, such as Sir Walter Raleigh and Sir Philip Sidney, were talented amateurs whose official duties at court lay elsewhere. On the other hand, writers such as Edmund Spenser were professionals who had to depend on the support of the queen and other nobles to earn their keep.

A Royal Performance?

According to one story of doubtful authenticity, Queen Elizabeth once not only attended a performance of a Shakespeare play at one of the famous theaters south of London, but also even went onstage.

The best seats in the house were literally on the stage and off to one side. They were especially popular with male courtiers who liked to show off the fine clothes they were wearing.

The story goes that the queen, while occupying one of these seats, grew so bored with the performance that she got up and strolled leisurely through the actors to the other side. When the actors ignored her and carried on with the play, she walked back across and dropped a glove at Shakespeare's feet.

The playwright supposedly picked it up, offered it to the queen with a flourish, and said, "And though now bent on this high embassy/Yet stoop we to take up our Cousin's glove," whereupon the audience burst out in applause.

The story, which is found in *All the Queen's Men* by Peter Brimacombe, is very improbable. Elizabeth would have been extremely unlikely to have gone to a public theater. When she saw plays, they were usually brought to the palace or performed in the houses of great nobles.

Elizabeth loved plays and especially enjoyed bawdy comedies. Here, the queen (in box at center) views a performance of Shakespeare's comedy The Merry Wives of Windsor.

Not all members of the court, however, were strong patrons of the arts. For example, William Cecil, when told by the queen to pay Spenser £100 for a collection of poems, groused, "What! All this for a song?"[115]

The Court Fools

Entertainment of a less refined sort was provided by court jesters, or fools, as they were commonly known. Elizabeth had several during her reign, but her favorite and easily the most famous was Dick Tarleton, who was adept at reading the queen's moods and knew just what to say to lift her spirits. Her courtiers knew this and sometimes employed him to soften Elizabeth up before they sought some favor. Dr. Thomas Fuller, writing in the next century, related that when the queen

> was serious (I dare not say sullen) and out of good humour, he [Tarleton] could un-dumpish her at his pleasure. Her highest Favourites, would in some Cases, go to Tarleton, before they would go to the Queen, and he was their Usher to prepare their advantageous access unto Her. In a word, He told the Queen more of her faults, than most of her

79

Chaplains, and cured her Melancholy better than all of her physicians.[116]

Jugglers, acrobats, and other such entertainers performed for the court. Robert Laneham, in his account of Elizabeth's progress to Dudley's estate at Kenilworth, described an Italian contortionist who put on a show "with sundry windings, gyrings and circumflexions; all so lightly and with such ease as by me, in a few words, it is not expressible by pen or speech. . . . [I] began to doubt whether it was a man or a spirit [with a back] metalled like a lamprey, that has no bone, but a line like a lute string."[117]

Sometimes the members of the court would amuse themselves with card, board, or dice games, often gambling much more than they could afford to lose. Playing cards with Elizabeth herself could be especially expensive, since she did not like to lose and her opponents usually saw to it that she did not. Her

The Wicked Theater

The upright merchants of London frowned on the theater, since it tended to distract people from work and worship. This passage is from an act of the City of London council in 1574. It is found in The Horizon Book of the Elizabethan World *by Lacey Baldwin Smith.*

Sundry great disorders and inconveniences have been found to ensue to this city by the inordinate haunting of great multitudes of people, especially youth, to plays, interludes, shows—namely, occasion of frays and quarrels; evil practices of incontinency in great inns have chambers and secret places adjoining to their open stages and galleries; inveigling and alluring of maids, specially orphans and good citizens' children under age, to privy and unmet contacts; the publishing of unchaste, uncomely, and unshamefast speeches and doings; withdrawing of the queen's majesty's subjects from divine service on Sundays and holidays, at which times such plays were chiefly used; unthrifty waste of the money of the poor and found persons; sundry robberies by picking and cutting of purses; uttering of popular, busy, and seditious matters; and many other corruptions of youth and other enormities—besides that also sundry slaughters and mayhemings of the queen's subjects have happened by ruins of scaffolds, frames, and stages, and by engines, weapons, and powder used in plays.

favorite card game was one called primero, and one of her frequent opponents was Lord North. His household accounts show regular entries of sums as large as £70, about $10,000, "lost to the queen at play."[118]

Physical Skills

Elizabeth's courtiers were expected to have more than elegance and wit. Physical skills also were prized. The queen's tutor, Roger Ascham, urged young men

> to ride comely, to run fair at the tilt or ring [trying to hit a target with a lance while on horseback], to play at all weapons, to shoot fair in bow, or surely in gun; to vault lustily, to run, to leap, to wrestle, to swim . . . to hawk, to hunt, to play at tennis, and all pastimes generally which be joined with labour, used in open place, and on the day light, containing either some fit exercise for war, or some pleasant pastime for peace.[119]

Tilting, or jousting, had been used for centuries to keep men fit and skilled for warfare. By the time of the Tudors, firearms had made the mounted knight obsolete in actual battle, but jousting survived as a sport largely because the nobility loved the pageantry associated with tournaments and men enjoyed displaying their prowess and their magnificent suits of armor.

Tilting served two purposes other than pure sport. First, it gave men a method to prove their military skills and courage without actually going to war, which the queen despised as a waste of both money and men. Second, tournaments furnished a safe outlet for romantic inclinations. There were many more eligible men at court than women, but the code of chivalry that surrounded tournaments allowed men to act toward women in the roles of protectors—to display affection for them as ideals of beauty and virtue, without the complications of actual physical involvement.

Fencing

For those who could not afford horses and armor, fencing was popular. As with much else, elegance was the rule. Instead of the massive broadsword and buckler (a small, round shield), men adopted the long, slim rapier, which was seen as much more fashionable. The change was not popular with everyone. Playwright Henry Porter complained, "Sword and buckler fight begin to grow out of use. I am sorry for it. I shall never see good manhood again. If it be once gone, this poking fight with rapier and dagger will come up. Then the tall man will be spitted like a cat or rabbit."[120]

While tilting and fencing were for men only, both sexes enjoyed hunting. The English nobility had been passionately fond of deer hunting for centuries, and huge sections of forest were reserved for their use. So seriously did the kings treasure their deer that the poor man who killed one in a royal forest to feed his family faced the death penalty.

A knight kneels at a jousting tournament. The sport was popular with the nobility because of its pageantry and because it involved displays of manly strength.

One type of deer hunting was the chase, in which a deer was flushed from hiding by dogs and pursued on horseback until it fell exhausted. The first hunter to reach the animal would then kill it by slitting its throat.

Elizabeth was an enthusiastic hunter, riding to the chase when she was well into her sixties. Throughout most of her later years, however, she hunted in more comfort from a small pavilion. Servants, beating the bushes with sticks and making loud noise, would drive the deer toward the pavilion, where the queen and her company waited with crossbows.

Falconry and hawking were gentler forms of hunting and ones especially enjoyed by the Maids of Honor, each of whom had her own birds. They would ride forth with the queen, their birds on their arms, waiting for game birds to be flushed from bushes. They then let loose their falcons or hawks, which soared high above their prey, then swooped down for the kill.

Undercurrent of Cruelty

The pleasures of Elizabeth's court were marked by an undercurrent of cruelty. Nowhere was this more evident than in the enjoyment courtiers found in the blood sports, such as cockfighting and bearbaiting or bullbaiting. Cockfighting pitted two roosters against one another, fighting to the death with sharp blades attached to their feet.

An accomplished horsewoman, Elizabeth enjoyed hunting from horseback.

Bears and bulls were the animals most often "baited," being held by a length of chain to a stake while they were attacked by a pack of dogs, usually bulldogs or mastiffs. The dogs would circle around the larger animal, looking for an opportunity to rush in and take hold with their strong jaws before they could be clawed or gored. The dogs won if the larger animal was killed. They lost if so many of them were killed or disabled that the rest refused to attack.

This sort of bloody spectacle, excessively violent and cruel by modern standards, fascinated Elizabeth and her court. Laneham described a bearbaiting at Kenilworth, admitting to feeling a "goodly relief" to see how the bear "with biting, with clawing, with roaring, tossing and tumbling, would work himself free . . . at such expense of blood and leather."[121]

Not everyone, however, found the blood sports so attractive. The Puritans condemned them, as they condemned so many of the pastimes of the nobility. Writing in 1583, the Puritan comentator Philip Stubbes asked, "What Christian heart can take pleasure to see one poor beast to rend, tear and kill another, all for his foolish pleasure."[122]

Cruel blood sports such as bearbaiting were a source of fascination to the queen and her court.

The sports and amusements of Elizabeth and her court were reflections of the nation itself—proud, bold, and boisterous. England had emerged from under the shadow of larger, more powerful neighbors and was beginning to acquire that sense of self-confidence—some would call it arrogance—that would mark the future British Empire. As historians A.L. Rowse and George Harrison wrote, "The fact was that they [the Elizabethans] were a sort of children. The age was young; they had all the braggadocio and lack of restraint of a magnificent, bounding youth."[123]

The Court on Display

The adage that clothes make the man—or woman—was never more demonstrated than at the court of Elizabeth I. The key to success was being noticed by the right people, and the key to getting noticed was to dress as fashionably and expensively as possible. In few societies has clothing been so important as a symbol of status or would-be status. As the queen's godson, John Harrington, put it, "We goe brave in apparell that wee may be taken for better men that wee bee."[124]

The extravagance in costume was a reflection of the general exuberance of the age. Long on the margins of European affairs, both geographically and politically, England assumed more

significance as a result of the Protestant Reformation and the exploration of the New World. England was becoming a world power, and the pride of the people was shown in their dress.

Dress was such an indicator of one's class that regulations known as sumptuary laws were passed in an attempt to keep people from dressing above their station. The law recognized nine levels of society, the highest consisting of dukes, marquises, earls, and barons and the lowest consisting of servants. However, the laws, which defined which materials could be used in clothes worn by each class, were difficult to enforce, and punishments, in the form of fines, were very rare. As Harrington wrote,

Our zealous preachers that would pride repress,

Complain against Apparells great excess,

For though the laws against yt are express,

Each lady like a Queen herself doth dress,

A merchaunt's wife like to a baroness.[125]

An Unwary Bishop

Zealous preachers did, indeed, complain about the extravagance in dress, but few in the court paid any attention, knowing how fond Elizabeth was of stylish clothes, both for herself and those around her. The bishop of London once was foolish enough to preach on "the vanitie of decking the body too finely" when the queen was present. She promptly walked out of the service, saying, "If the bishope helde more discourse on such matters she woold fitte him for heaven."[126]

The queen set the standard for fashion just as she did for much else. She considered the elegance of her person just as important in portraying a regal image as the elegance of her court. Her wardrobe was said to contain more than two thousand

---

The Clerical Complaint

Not only Puritans, but also clergy of the Church of England condemned things they considered worldly, and few things aroused their contempt more than extravagant dress. Bishop Pilkington of Durham preached against the cost of such finery, but probably not within Queen Elizabeth's hearing. This excerpt from a sermon is found in Memoirs of the Court of Elizabeth *by Lucy Aikin.*

These tender [courtiers] must have one gown for the day, another for the night; one long, another short; one for winter; another for summer. One furred through, another but faced; one for the work-day, another for the holiday. One of this color, another of that. One of cloth, another of silk, or damask; change of apparel; one afore dinner, another at after: one of Spanish fashion, another of Turkey. And to be brief, never content with enough, but always devising new fashions and strange. Yea, a ruffian will have more in his ruff and his hose than he should spend in a year: he which ought to go in a russet [plain] coat, spends as much on apparel for him and his wife, as his father would have kept a good house with.

gowns with the accompanying accessories. Supposedly, she never wore the same costume twice, although the costly material sometimes was reused in a different style.

Rich fabric was hardly enough for the queen. It had to be embroidered with silver and gold thread and decorated with pearls, diamonds, or other precious stones. Indeed, the combination of jewel-decked gowns and lively dancing led to some expensive losses. The household accounts show lengthy lists with entries like "Lost, at Richmond . . . from her Majesty's back, wearing the gown of purple cloth of silver, one great diamond out of a clasp of gold."[127]

Women's dress was nowhere near as extravagant at the start of Elizabeth's reign as in later years. Spanish influence was strong in Queen Mary's court, meaning that most clothes were severe in cut and somber in color. After Elizabeth became queen, the court became a much livelier place and colors brightened as well. Eventually, materials were dyed every imaginable color, with imaginative names to match—pease porridge tawny, dead Spaniard, popingay blue, lady's blush, lusty gallant, devil-in-the-hedge.

Colors were important to the Elizabethans, who loved symbolism, and were intended to reflect the emotions of the wearer. Black meant grief, much as it would in future times, but yellow meant hope; green, love; blue, friendship; orange, deception; red, power; turquoise, jealousy. In addition, colors could be used in combination to send a more complex

Elizabeth's sense of fashion and style contributed to her regal image and influenced the dress of members of her court.

message. For instance, yellow and black worn together meant sadness at the departure of someone close.

A Lengthy Process

Dressing a woman of Elizabeth's court was a considerable production. As a character in a play of the time said, "A ship is sooner rigged than a gentlewoman made ready."[128] The comparison to a ship, with its many sails held in place by an array of ropes, was apt. The typical costume consisted of many garments in many pieces, and all had to be tied, laced, and hooked together.

The kirtle and gown were the basic components of women's dress. The kirtle had two parts, the skirt and bodice, the name coming from the two "bodies," worn over the front and back of the upper torso and joined at the sides. The front part of the bodice was tight fitting and tapered to a point at the waist. It could have either a high or low neckline. If it was low, the woman could choose to leave her upper bosom bare or cover it with jewelry or a cloth garment called the partlet.

Farthingales

Skirts were full and floor-length, but during Elizabeth's reign grew from simple cone shapes to vast billows of material. Skirts were draped over farthingales, a series of linked hoops made of bone, wire, or wood that increased in circumference as they went from the waist to the feet. Material was stretched over the hoops to form a shape for the skirt. Late in the reign, the bell-shaped farthingale gave way to the wheel style, in which the skirt was taken out at a right angle to the waist for a distance of up to four feet before falling straight to the floor.

To provide a balance for the size of skirts, women wore large, padded sleeves that, because of their shape, were called leg-of-mutton. These usually were separate from the bodice and sometimes of a different material. The sleeves were tied on and the ties were hidden by padded rolls on each shoulder that became increasingly decorative, sometimes with velvet bows.

The gown was worn over the kirtle and could be either open (or "loose") or

The Virtue of Extravagance

There were practical reasons for a person in Elizabethan times to dress as finely as possible. Playwright Ben Jonson, in Every Man Out of His Humour, *gave a few in this excerpt found in* Dress in the Age of Elizabeth *by Jane Ashelford.*

Rich apparel has strange virtues; it makes him that hath it without means [poor] esteemed for an excellent wit; he that enjoys it with means puts the world in remembrance of his means; it helps the deformities of nature, and gives luster to her beauties; makes continual holyday where it shines; sets the wits of ladies at work, that otherwise would be idle; furnisheth your two-shilling ordinary [a complete meal costing about six dollars at an inn]; takes possession of your stage at your new play.

closed. The loose gown hung from the shoulders and fell naturally over the skirt. Closed gowns were fitted to the waist, where they were attached to the skirt, then fell in folds over the skirt. Gowns were not worn at all times, but usually for warmth or on formal occasions.

The Ruff

The most distinctive feature of dress in the court—for both women and men— was the ruff. Ruffs began as edgings of frill attached to the top of a high collar. They eventually would become separate pieces and grow to enormous proportions, typical of the exaggerations in style that marked the era. A later writer, Horace Walpole, summed up Elizabethan women's dress as "vast ruff, vaster farthingale and a bushel of pearls."[129]

Ruffs were made from lace and at first were held in place by wire "supportasses." These gave way in the 1560s to a new method, starching, brought to England by a Mrs. Dinghen from the Netherlands, who soon grew wealthy teaching her technique to eager students at £5 a lesson. The material was dipped into starch, then arranged—a task that sometimes took hours—on steel or silver "poking sticks" to dry. While earlier ruffs were worn open at the front, they were tied together in later years to form a thick, white plate that appeared to separate completely the head from the rest of the body.

In the later years of the reign, ruffs grew huge, reaching a diameter of more than two feet and were arranged in intri-

The ruff was a distinctive part of dress during the Elizabethan period. As the years passed, the style became exaggerated, resulting in ruffs more than two feet in diameter.

cate loops and layers. Like most everything else about court dress, they drew criticism from Puritans like Philip Stubbes, who found solace in the fact that they were vulnerable to the unpredictable English weather and, when caught in the rain, would "goe flip flap in the winde, like rags flying abroad, and lye on their [courtiers'] shoulders like the dishcoulte of a slut."[130]

The Stomacher

Another piece of women's apparel that came under criticism, both from the Puritans and physicians of the day, was the stomacher. This was a triangle of stiffened material attached to the bodice that tapered to a point below the waist. The stomacher compressed the abdomen to such an extent that doctors worried that they might hurt women's ability to bear children. Such warnings did little, however, to stop women from seeking the fashionably tiny waist that stomachers provided.

There were more—many more—articles of clothing that went to make up a woman's costume. Smocks of fine linen were worn under the kirtle to protect the skin and to protect the kirtle from perspiration. Petticoats were worn under the skirts. Intricate lace collars were called bands. Hats of rich material were adorned with expensive feathers or jewels.

Silk stockings made their first appearance in England in 1559 when Mistress Montague, who made silk articles for Elizabeth, presented her with a pair as a New Year's present. When the queen expressed her delight, Mistress Montague said she would immediately begin work on additional pairs. "Do so," said Elizabeth, "for indeed I like silk stockings so well, because they are pleasant fine, and delicate, that henceforth I will weare no more cloth stockings."[131]

Women took pains to keep their faces just as attractive as their clothing and employed cosmetics liberally, usually in an effort to keep their skin fair and free of wrinkles. As she aged, Elizabeth turned more and more to various concoctions to try to retain a youthful appearance and also wore red-gold wigs to conceal her thinning hair. To whiten her skin, she used a mixture of egg white, powdered eggshell, alum, borax, and poppy seeds. Since she refused to use mirrors in the last decades of the reign, she could not see —or did not want to admit—how obvious her attempts were. In 1600 an observer wrote that her makeup was "in some places nearly half an inch thick."[132]

Men's Fashions

The extravagance of women's dress in Elizabeth's court was equaled, and perhaps even exceeded, by that of the men. Men competed with one another in an endless chase after the latest and most exaggerated fashions. A foreign observer, Emanuel van Meteren, noted that the men "are very inconsistent and desirous of novelties, changing their fashions every year to the astonishment of many."[133]

If the men of the court changed their fashions every year, they tried to change their costumes every day. They had not only to reach, but also to maintain, the height of fashion in order to avoid the impression that their fortunes had diminished. A new outfit could not be of lesser quality than the old ones, and the new ones—once worn—could not be worn again lest others think the wearer could not afford new clothes.

Elizabeth's court was not the only place for the stylish man to be seen. Those who had not yet gained entrance to the court would "publish" their clothes by parading up and down the central aisle of St. Paul's Cathedral between 10 A.M. and noon. Two full cir-

Men of the court were as obsessed with fashion as the women. Courtiers like the dapper gentleman pictured here would appear in a different outfit each day.

cuits were thought to be sufficient; any more, and the onlookers might tire of the new outfit. Tailors took advantage of the fashion show, lurking behind pillars to take notes and make drawings so that they could dash back to their shops to copy the latest trends.

Dressing was just as laborious and lengthy a task for a man as it was for a woman. His servant would first slip on the embroidered shirt, which had been warmed in front of a fire, followed by a waistcoat or vest on top of which were placed the doublet and hose, topped off by a cloak. The ruff had to be attached to the doublet, and finally, a girdle (or belt), for carrying a dagger and sword was buckled around the waist.

Doublet and Hose

The essential parts of a man's costume were the doublet and hose. Hose was the name given to both the piece of clothing worn around the waist to midthigh and those worn on the legs. Before 1570 the upper hose, or "trunkhose," were sewn to the stockings, but later they became separate pieces that had to be laced together. The most popular style of trunkhose was the Spanish kettledrum, which swelled out from the waist then back into the thigh in a round shape. The entire garment was stuffed with material called bombast to hold its shape and was often made in panels of alternating colors or materials with a rich lining.

By the 1580s the trunkhose had shrunk to a pad around the hips, below which were canions, tubular extensions that extended to each knee. Below the trunkhose or canions, depending on which style was worn, were the stockings, or "netherhose." These could extend all the way up to the trunkhose, to which they would be laced, or just over the knee to the canion, in which case they were held in place by a garter.

Yet another form of hose were breeches, which were fuller and longer than trunkhose. Breeches came in many styles. Ventians could be full or shaped and were closed at the knee with ties or buckles. Baggy breeches open at the knee were called galligaskins, while the baggy variety closed at the knee were known as slops.

The doublet was a tight-fitting garment that covered the upper torso. It could be worn either with or without sleeves. The sleeves could be made of the same or a contrasting material and fastened to the body of the doublet by ties. Rich satin or velvet lined the inside of the doublet, and the lining was exposed by "slashing" or "pinking" the outer material to allow the inner finery to show.

Doublets had many styles and shapes, but most tapered sharply from the shoulders to the waist, coming to a point in front. The front of the doublet was padded with bombast. This padding grew over the years to the point where the doublet bellied out in front then curved back in below the waist. This so-called peascod style was highly fashionable, yet highly restrictive. The Puritan Stubbes claimed that men who wore this style were so confined that they could hardly stoop or lie down, "soe styffe and sturdy they [the doublets] stand about them."[134]

Jerkins and Cloaks

A jerkin was sometimes worn over the doublet. This was an outer vest, sleeved or sleeveless, fastened down the center. It was often covered with embroidery.

The cloak was the most expensive part of a gentleman's wardrobe. They were made of costly materials, heavily embroidered, edged with fur, and lined with the same rich fabrics as the doublet. The story of Sir Walter Raleigh spreading

his cloak for Queen Elizabeth to walk upon is intended to represent a supreme sacrifice on Raleigh's part.

Styles of cloaks changed just as often as styles of doublets. The Spanish cloak had a hood and was very short. The Dutch cloak had no hood, but had wide sleeves and featured a "guard," a highly decorated border. The French cloak, either short or long depending on the fashion of the decade, was worn over the left shoulder and fastened under the arm.

Men's hats were just as showy as those worn by women. Beaver pelt was the favorite material, with the crown surrounded by a hatband sometimes fash-

William Shakespeare is pictured here wearing a doublet in the peascod style. The front of such garments was thickly padded, restricting the wearer's movements.

The Changeable Cloak

Some of the most observant comments on Elizabethan dress came from the Puritan writer Philip Stubbes. In this passage, found in Dress in the Age of Elizabeth, *by Jane Ashelford, he talks about the constant changes in the styles of men's cloaks:.*

Cloakes of diverse and sundry colours, white, red, tawnie, black, greene, yellowe, russet, purple, violet, and infinite other colours: some of cloth, silk, velvet, taffetie and such like, whereof some be of the Spanish, French and Dutch fashion. These cloakes must be guarded [richly bordered], laced and thoroughly faced; and sometimes so lined as the inner side standeth almost in as much as the outer side; some have sleeves, other some have none; some have hoodes to pull over the head, some have none; some are hanged with points and tassels of gold, silver or silk, some without all this.

A member of the nobility wears a luxurious cloak, considered the height of fashion at Elizabeth's court.

ioned entirely out of pearls or jewels. Feathers topped the hats, most often ostrich feathers that could be dyed to match the rest of the outfit. Ostrich feathers were popular not only for their appearance, but also because they were a show of wealth. A single feather cost as much as a laborer would earn in a week.

The Cost of Style

The constant demand for new and more fashionable clothes was, indeed, extremely expensive. It was not unusual for an ambitious newcomer to spend all he had—and more—on his clothes. Playwright Christopher Marlowe wrote about the dandy who "wears a lord's revenue upon his back."[135] When Arthur Throckmorton, brother-in-law of Sir Walter Raleigh, came to court in 1583, he financed his wardrobe by selling much of his land and borrowing heavily from his brother. And Ben Jonson, in his play *Every Man Out of His Humour,* has a character tell another that he "turned four or five hundred acres of your best land into two or three trunks of apparel."[136]

One way to avoid the high cost of clothing was simply not to pay for it. Indeed, it was considered somewhat demeaning to pay a tailor promptly. In another Elizabethan play, one man tells another that he has not paid for his clothes "to keepe the fashion: it's your onely fashion now of your best ranke of gallants, to make their tailors waite for their money."[137]

Wearing One's Feelings

Like women, men used colors to proclaim their emotions. In addition, embroidery on a person's clothing told much about his or her mood. If a person's love was not returned, he or she might wear something showing an eye shedding a tear or a heart pierced by an arrow. Someone waiting for a loved one to return from a journey might have hourglasses covering a dress or cloak. Each embroidered flower had a meaning. The lily, for example, meant purity.

Elizabeth loved symbolism of this sort as much as anyone. One portrait shows her wearing a representation of the phoenix. This mythical bird could reproduce itself only by burning and rising from its own ashes. For Elizabeth, therefore, the phoenix represented chastity, since sex was not part of its life cycle. She also was painted with the figure of a pelican, symbolic of sacrifice since the mother pelican supposedly will peck her own breast to feed her blood to her chicks.

Such fanciful adornments, combined with the richness of materials and the constant revolution in style, made the court dress of Elizabeth's reign one of the most unusual and individualistic of any in European history. The Elizabethan nobility were proud of themselves and displayed their pride in the extravagance of their dress. Two years after Elizabeth's death, a keen observer, looking over some portraits, commented, "When your posterity shall see our pictures they shall think we were foolishly proud of apparell."[138]

Epilogue:
Faded but
Not Forgotten

Queen Elizabeth was the sun around which not only her court but also her entire country revolved. At length, however, the sun began to set and the shadows lengthened. There was gaiety and merriment, but it seemed forced and false, much like the praises of youthful beauty heaped upon the wrinkled old woman on the throne. Yet, while the brilliance that was Elizabeth's court finally faded, it could never be completely extinguished.

Elizabeth never fully recovered from the rebellion by her favorite, the earl of Essex, or from his execution for treason in 1601. Death had claimed all those people closest to her—Cecil, Dudley, Hatton—and she knew it was closing in on her. When someone tried to cheer her up, she replied, "I am tied with a chain of iron about my neck. I am tied, I am tied, and the case is altered with me."[139]

The drama of Queen Mary's death and Elizabeth's own accession played out again. Just as courtiers had deserted her half sister, so too did more and more people turn their thoughts northward to the heir apparent to the throne, King James VI of Scotland, son of Elizabeth's old rival, Mary, Queen of Scots.

Death of Elizabeth

Finally, on March 24, 1603, she died peacefully in her sleep. She was sixty-nine years old and had reigned over England for almost forty-five years. They had been great years for England, and Elizabeth and her court had both inspired and been creations of that greatness. Queen, court, and country had been bold to the point of rashness, confident to the point of arrogance, self-indulgent to the point of extravagance. Yet, the court had motivated writers, artists, and scientists; the daring explorations of the time had made the court—and the country—wealthy.

The court's glitter did not blind everyone. The lavish displays unleashed a correspondingly strong reaction from the Puritans. They condemned almost everything about the court—sports, dress, holidays—as opposite to the sober and righteous life they said God wanted people to live. Ironically, it was the relative religious tolerance of Elizabeth's reign that gave Puritanism the freedom to flourish and grow.

The grandeur that had been Elizabeth's court did not long outlive Elizabeth. The courts of James Stuart, who became James I of England, and his son, Charles I, were splendid, but they no longer embodied the soul of the country. These kings believed they ruled by the express will of God. So had Elizabeth, but there had been a difference. She accepted as part of God's will a responsibility to serve and care for those she ruled. James and Charles thought the people existed to serve them, and thus they never had the people's love.

The Puritan Victory

As a result, the ruler and the ruled grew steadily apart in the first half of the 1600s. The excesses of the court were no longer compensated for by the affection and respect for the monarch as in Elizabeth's day. Eventually, the Puritans and others had their way. A bloody civil war resulted in the execution of Charles I and a period of more than a decade during which England had no king.

England, however, never forgot what it had been under Elizabeth. The people soon tired of strict Puritan rule, and the monarchy was restored in 1660. The brightness of Elizabeth and the court was rekindled in the minds of English of all classes. The years of Good Queen Bess were a lantern lighting the way to future greatness, and the country, indeed, went on to form

Almost seventy years old, the indomitable Elizabeth died peacefully as she slept.

the strongest empire the world has ever known.

Elizabeth and the men and women of her court stirred the imaginations of generations who came after them, encouraging in them the same robust spirit of adventure and conquest. As historian William Camden wrote in the next century, "No Oblivion shall ever bury the Glory of her Name, for her happy and renowned Memory still liveth, and shall for ever live in the Minds of men to all Posterity."[140]

Notes

Introduction: The One Sun

1. Quoted in Susan Watkins, *In Public and Private: Elizabeth I and Her World*. New York: Thames and Hudson, 1998, p. 149.
2. Quoted in Alfred L. Rowse and George B. Harrison, *Queen Elizabeth and Her Subjects*. Freeport, NY: Books for Libraries Press, 1935, p. 96.
3. Quoted in Ian Dunlop, *Palaces and Progresses of Elizabeth I*. New York: Taplinger, 1970, p. 77.
4. Quoted in Ralph Dutton, *English Court Life from Henry VII to George II*. London: B.T. Batsford, 1963, p. 66.

Chapter 1: Gloriana

5. Quoted in Carolly Erickson, *The First Elizabeth*. New York: Summit, 1983, p. 20.
6. Quoted in Mary M. Luke, *Gloriana: The Years of Elizabeth I*. New York: Coward, McCann & Geohagen, 1973, p. 29.
7. Quoted in Violet Wilson, *Queen Elizabeth's Maids of Honour*. London: John Lane, 1922, p. 4.
8. Quoted in Elizabeth Jenkins, *Elizabeth the Great*. New York: Capricorn Books, 1958, p. 31.
9. Quoted in Rowse and Harrison, *Queen Elizabeth and Her Subjects,* p. 22.
10. Quoted in Erickson, *The First Elizabeth*, p. 134.
11. Quoted in Jenkins, *Elizabeth the Great*, p. 60.
12. Quoted in Luke, *Gloriana*, p. 32.
13. Quoted in Erickson, *The First Elizabeth*, p. 179.
14. Quoted in Watkins, *In Public and Private*, p. 45.
15. Quoted in Lisa Hopkins, *Queen Elizabeth I and Her Court*. London: Vision Press, 1990, p. 137.
16. Quoted in Luke, *Gloriana*, p. 36.
17. Quoted in Erickson, *The First Elizabeth*, p. 178.
18. Peter Brimacombe, *All the Queen's Men: The World of Elizabeth I*. New York: St. Martin's Press, p. 48.

Chapter 2: The Queen's Majesty

19. Quoted in David Starkey et al. *The English Court: from the Wars of the Roses to the Civil War*. London: Longman, 1987, p. 74.
20. Quoted in Brimacombe, *All the Queen's Men,* p. 49.
21. Quoted in Brimacombe, *All the Queen's Men,* p. 29.

22. Quoted in Wilson, *Queen Elizabeth's Maids of Honour*, p. 3.
23. Quoted in Wilson, *Queen Elizabeth's Maids of Honour*, p. 200.
24. Quoted in Wilson, *Queen Elizabeth's Maids of Honour*, p. 199.
25. Quoted in Brimacombe, *All the Queen's Men*, p. 57.
26. Quoted in Erickson, *The First Elizabeth*, p. 350.
27. Quoted in Dutton, *English Court Life from Henry VII to George II*, p. 163.
28. Quoted in Edith Sitwell, *The Queens and the Hive*. Boston: Little, Brown, 1962, p. 48.
29. Quoted in Lucy Aikin, *Memoirs of the Court of Elizabeth, Queen of England*. London: Ward, Lock, 1875, p. 384.
30. Quoted in Brimacombe, *All the Queen's Men*, p. 19.
31. Quoted in Dutton, *English Court Life from Henry VII to George II*, p. 81.
32. Quoted in Rachel and Allen Percival, *The Court of Elizabeth the First*. London: Stainer and Bell, 1976, p. 75.

Chapter 3: All the Queen's Men

33. Quoted in Sitwell, *The Queens and the Hive*, p. 86.
34. Quoted in Wilson, *Queen Elizabeth's Maids of Honour*, p. 217.
35. Quoted in Dutton, *English Court Life from Henry VII to George II*, p. 66.
36. Quoted in Watkins, *In Public and Private*, p. 164.
37. Quoted in Luke, *Gloriana*, p. 85.
38. Quoted in Aiken, *Memoirs of the Court of Elizabeth*, p. 143.
39. Quoted in Luke, *Gloriana*, p. 67.
40. Quoted in Luke, *Gloriana*, p. 51.
41. Quoted in Erickson, *The First Elizabeth*, p. 188.
42. Quoted in Luke, *Gloriana*, p. 121.
43. Quoted in Wilson, *Queen Elizabeth's Maids of Honour*, p. 136.
44. Quoted in Frederick Chamberlin, *The Private Character of Queen Elizabeth*. New York: Dodd, Mead, 1922, p. 249.
45. Quoted in Wilson, *Queen Elizabeth's Maids of Honour*, p. 167.
46. Quoted in Chamberlin, *The Private Character of Queen Elizabeth*, p. 252.
47. Quoted in Chamberlin, *The Private Character of Queen Elizabeth*, p. 152.
48. Quoted in Aiken, *Memoirs of the Court of Elizabeth*, p. 132.
49. Quoted in Jenkins, *Elizabeth the Great*, p. 207.
50. Quoted in Erickson, *The First Elizabeth*, p. 312.
51. Quoted in Wallace MacCaffrey, *Elizabeth I*. London: Edward Arnold, 1993, p. 361.

Chapter 4: All the Queen's Women

52. Quoted in Rowse and Harrison, *Queen Elizabeth and Her Subjects*, p. 94.

53. Quoted in Anne Somerset, *Ladies-in-Waiting: From the Tudors to the Present Day*. New York: Alfred A. Knopf, 1984, p. 70.

54. Quoted in Luke, *Gloriana*, p. 187.

55. Quoted in Somerset, *Ladies-in-Waiting*, p. 66.

56. Quoted in Wilson, *Queen Elizabeth's Maids of Honour*, p. 227.

57. Quoted in Wilson, *Queen Elizabeth's Maids of Honour*, p. 13.

58. Quoted in Somerset, *Ladies-in-Waiting*, p. 64.

59. Quoted in Aiken, *Memoirs of the Court of Elizabeth*, p. 318.

60. Quoted in Wilson, *Queen Elizabeth's Maids of Honour*, p. 107.

61. Quoted in Somerset, *Ladies-in-Waiting*, p. 89.

62. Quoted in Wilson, *Queen Elizabeth's Maids of Honour*, p. 32.

63. Quoted in Somerset, *Ladies-in-Waiting*, p. 91.

64. Quoted in Wilson, *Queen Elizabeth's Maids of Honour*, p. 41.

65. Quoted in Somerset, *Ladies-in-Waiting*, p. 61.

Chapter 5: The Court at Home

66. Quoted in Dunlop, *Palaces and Progresses of Elizabeth I*, p. 37.

67. Quoted in Watkins, *In Public and Private*, p. 147.

68. Quoted in Dunlop, *Palaces and Progresses of Elizabeth I*, p. 23.

69. Quoted in Dunlop, *Palaces and Progresses of Elizabeth I*, p. 79.

70. Quoted in Dunlop, *Palaces and Progresses of Elizabeth I*, p. 79.

71. Quoted in Dunlop, *Palaces and Progresses of Elizabeth I*, p. 69.

72. Quoted in Dunlop, *Palaces and Progresses of Elizabeth I*, p. 70.

73. Quoted in Sitwell, *The Queens and the Hive*, p. 85.

74. Quoted in Dunlop, *Palaces and Progresses of Elizabeth I*, p. 51.

75. Quoted in Dunlop, *Palaces and Progresses of Elizabeth I*, p. 60.

76. Quoted in Dunlop, *Palaces and Progresses of Elizabeth I*, p. 59.

77. Quoted in Dunlop, *Palaces and Progresses of Elizabeth I*, p. 33.

78. Quoted in Dunlop, *Palaces and Progresses of Elizabeth I*, p. 60.

79. Quoted in Dunlop, *Palaces and Progresses of Elizabeth I*, p. 66.

80. Quoted in Watkins, *In Public and Private*, p. 96.

81. Quoted in Dunlop, *Palaces and Progresses of Elizabeth I*, p. 97.

82. Quoted in Dunlop, *Palaces and Progresses of Elizabeth I*, p. 107.

83. Quoted in Dunlop, *Palaces and Progresses of Elizabeth I*, p. 112.

84. Quoted in Watkins, *In Public and Private*, p. 66.

85. Quoted in Dunlop, *Palaces and Progresses of Elizabeth I*, p. 110.

86. Quoted in Dunlop, *Palaces and Progresses of Elizabeth I*, p. 28.

87. Quoted in Neville Williams, *The Life and Times of Elizabeth I*. Garden City, NY: Doubleday, 1972, p. 136.

Chapter 6: The Court on the Move

88. Quoted in Watkins, *In Public and Private*, p. 56.

89. Quoted in Mary Hill Cole, *The Portable Queen: Elizabeth I and the Politics of Ceremony*. Amherst: University of Massachusetts Press, 1999, p. 65.

90. Quoted in Dunlop, *Palaces and Progresses of Elizabeth I*, p. 115.

91. Quoted in Dunlop, *Palaces and Progresses of Elizabeth I*, p. 119.

92. Quoted in Dunlop, *Palaces and Progresses of Elizabeth I*, p. 128.

93. Quoted in Dunlop, *Palaces and Progresses of Elizabeth I*, p. 180.

94. Quoted in Dunlop, *Palaces and Progresses of Elizabeth I*, p. 116.

95. Quoted in Wilson, *Queen Elizabeth's Maids of Honour*, p. 62.

96. Quoted in Cole, *The Portable Queen*, p. 46.

97. Quoted in Dunlop, *Palaces and Progresses of Elizabeth I*, p. 151.

98. Quoted in Dunlop, *Palaces and Progresses of Elizabeth I*, p. 135.

99. Quoted in Dunlop, *Palaces and Progresses of Elizabeth I*, p. 145.

100. Quoted in Cole, *The Portable Queen*, p. 35.

101. Quoted in Dunlop, *Palaces and Progresses of Elizabeth I*, p. 184.

102. Quoted in Dunlop, *Palaces and Progresses of Elizabeth I*, p. 168.

103. Quoted in Dunlop, *Palaces and Progresses of Elizabeth I*, p. 132.

104. Quoted in Aikin, *Memoirs of the Court of Elizabeth*, p. 293.

105. Quoted in Watkins, *In Public and Private*, p. 63.

106. Quoted in Alan Glover, ed., *Gloriana's Glass*. London: Nonesuch Press, 1953, p. 92.

107. Quoted in Glover, *Gloriana's Glass*, p. 93.

108. Quoted in Erickson, *The First Elizabeth*, p. 276.

Chapter 7: The Court at Play

109. Quoted in Brimacombe, *All the Queen's Men*, p. 33.

110. Quoted in Erickson, *The First Elizabeth*, p. 220.

111. Quoted in Wilson, *Queen Elizabeth's Maids of Honour*, p. 265.

112. Quoted in Chamberlin, *The Private Character of Queen Elizabeth*, p. 105.

113. Quoted in Brimacombe, *All the Queen's Men*, p. 177.

114. Quoted in Aikin, *Memoirs of the Court of Elizabeth*, p. 295.

115. Quoted in Brimacombe, *All the Queen's Men*, p. 179.

116. Quoted in John Southworth, *Fools and Jesters at the English Court*. Thrupp, England: Sutton, 1998, p. 116.

117. Quoted in Dunlop, *Palaces and Progresses of Elizabeth I*, p. 148.

118. Quoted in Wilson, *Queen Elizabeth's Maids of Honour*, p. 79.

119. Quoted in A.L. Rowse, *Elizabethan Renaissance: The Life of the Society.* New York: Charles Scribner's Sons, 1971, p. 106.
120. Quoted in Rowse, *The Elizabethan Renaissance: The Life of the Society,* p. 144.
121. Quoted in Dunlop, *Palaces and Progresses of Elizabeth I,* p. 147.
122. Quoted in Dunlop, *Palaces and Progresses of Elizabeth I,* p. 147.
123. Rowse and Harrison, *Queen Elizabeth and Her Subjects,* p. 133.

Chapter 8: The Court on Display

124. Quoted in Wilson, *Queen Elizabeth's Maids of Honour,* p. 149.
125. Quoted in Jane Ashelford, *Dress in the Age of Elizabeth.* New York: Holmes and Meier, 1988, p. 109.
126. Quoted in Dutton, *English Court Life from Henry VII to George II,* p. 86.
127. Quoted in Dutton, *English Court Life from Henry VII to George II,* p. 86.
128. Quoted in Ashelford, *Dress in the Age of Elizabeth,* p. 14.
129. Quoted in Ashelford, *Dress in the Age of Elizabeth,* p. 11.
130. Quoted in Ashelford, *Dress in the Age of Elizabeth,* p. 46.
131. Quoted in Wilson, *Queen Elizabeth's Maids of Honour,* p. 40.
132. Quoted in Ashelford, *Dress in the Age of Elizabeth,* p. 8.
133. Quoted in Ashelford, *Dress in the Age of Elizabeth,* p. 74.
134. Quoted in Ashelford, *Dress in the Age of Elizabeth,* p. 47.
135. Quoted in Wilson, *Queen Elizabeth's Maids of Honour,* p. 149.
136. Quoted in Ashelford, *Dress in the Age of Elizabeth,* p. 44.
137. Quoted in Ashelford, *Dress in the Age of Elizabeth,* p. 77.
138. Quoted in Ashelford, *Dress in the Age of Elizabeth,* p. 8.

Epilogue: Faded but Not Forgotten

139. Quoted in Jenkins, *Elizabeth the Great,* p. 323.
140. Quoted in Watkins, *In Public and Private,* p. 197.

For Further Reading

Books

Kathryn Lasky, *Elizabeth I: Red Rose of the House of Tudor, England, 1544*. New York: Scholastic, 1999. One of a series of fictionalized diaries of famous characters in history, this volume covers the year when Elizabeth was ten and eleven years old, before the death of her father, Henry VIII.

Carolyn Meyer, *Beware, Princess Elizabeth*. San Diego, CA: Harcourt, 2001. Highly readable fictional account of the dangers Elizabeth faced before becoming queen. Written for readers in grades five through eight.

Jeffrey L. Singman, *Daily Life in Elizabethan England*. Westport, CT: Greenwood Press, 1995. Highly entertaining book that goes beyond descriptions of everyday life to include such information as recipes, clothing patterns, and game rules.

Diane Stanley and Peter Vennema, *Good Queen Bess: The Story of Elizabeth I of England*. New York: Four Winds Press, 1990. A good, simply written biography with excellent color illustrations by Diane Stanley.

Jane Resh Thomas, *Behind the Mask: The Life of Queen Elizabeth I*. New York: Clarion, 1998. Brightly written biography for young readers, amply illustrated in both color and black and white. Chronology and brief descriptions of major characters are helpful.

Stephen White-Thompson, *Elizabeth I and Tudor England*. New York: The Bookwright Press, 1985. Part of the Life and Times series. Excellent overview that deals not only with Elizabeth's life and reign, but also with the changes occurring in England, including short chapters on religion, government, and court life.

Websites

The Official Web Site of the British Monarchy. (www.royal.gov.uk). In addition to short biographies of kings and queens dating from 757 to the present, this fascinating site gives information on members of the present royal family and the role of the monarchy, plus pictures of royal residences and art treasures.

Heather, Thomas, *The Life and Times of Queen Elizabeth I*, 2001. (www.elizabethi.org). Comprehensive site that details many facets of Elizabeth's life and reign. Includes a "who's who" section, bibliography, and even a guide to portrayals of Elizabeth in films and on television.

Works Consulted

Lucy Aikin, *Memoirs of the Court of Elizabeth, Queen of England*. London: Ward, Lock, 1875. This huge, highly detailed biography is very dated and can be slow going for modern readers but is packed with information about every aspect of the reign.

Jane Ashelford, *Dress in the Age of Elizabeth*. New York: Holmes and Meier, 1988. Very detailed and lavishly illustrated description of the dress of the Elizabethan era, from that worn by the queen to the humble garments of the poor.

Peter Brimacombe, *All the Queen's Men: The World of Elizabeth I*. New York: St. Martin's Press, 2000. Biographical information on the many men who played prominent roles during the reign. Not only courtiers, but also explorers, scientists, and writers are covered.

Frederick Chamberlin, *The Private Character of Queen Elizabeth*. New York: Dodd, Mead, 1922. Very unusual book that examines Elizabeth's medical condition and thoroughly delves into various charges against her, such as her supposed love affairs with Robert Dudley and Thomas Seymour.

Mary Hill Cole, *The Portable Queen: Elizabeth I and the Politics of Ceremony.* Amherst: University of Massachusetts Press, 1999. Thorough research is evident in this extremely detailed account of the famous progresses of Elizabeth I.

A.H. Dodd, *Elizabethan England*. New York: G.P. Putnam's Sons, 1973. Well-illustrated look at the various aspects of life and society in Elizabethan England.

Ian Dunlop, *Palaces and Progresses of Elizabeth I*. New York: Taplinger, 1970. Excellent description of Elizabeth's principal residences and lively accounts of her visits to the homes of some of her most well-known subjects.

Ralph Dutton, *English Court Life from Henry VII to George II*. London: B.T. Batsford, 1963. Traces the evolution of life and customs in England's royal court through almost three centuries of rulers.

Carolly Erickson, *The First Elizabeth*. New York: Summit, 1983. The author's Ph.D. in medieval history is evident in this scholarly yet entertaining biography of Elizabeth. Particularly helpful for researchers is the exhaustive index.

Alan Glover, ed., *Gloriana's Glass*. London: Nonesuch Press, 1953. Interesting collection of contemporary documents concerning Elizabeth I, including descriptions of the court and poetry written by and about the queen.

Lisa Hopkins, *Queen Elizabeth I and Her Court*. London: Vision Press, 1990. Excellent account that blends biographical information on Elizabeth with details of both the public face and inner workings of her court.

Joel Hurstfield and Alan G.R. Smith, eds., *Elizabethan People: State and Society*. New York: St. Martin's Press, 1972. A wonderful collection of excerpts from letters, speeches, acts of Parliament, and many other documents organized by topic and presenting a good picture of Elizabethan life.

Elizabeth Jenkins, *Elizabeth and Leicester*. New York: Coward-McCann, 1961. Lengthy, thorough, yet highly enjoyable study of the lengthy and often tumultuous relationship between Queen Elizabeth I and Robert Dudley, earl of Leicester.

———, *Elizabeth the Great*. New York: Capricorn Books, 1958. Outstanding biography of Elizabeth I; the examination of her personal life is particularly revealing.

Mary M. Luke, *Gloriana: The Years of Elizabeth I*. New York: Coward, McCann & Geohagen, 1973. Third in a series that also includes works on Catherine of Aragon and Elizabeth I's early life. This book concentrates on the queen's life after she ascended to the throne.

Wallace MacCaffrey, *Elizabeth I*. London: Edward Arnold, 1993. Massive, very scholarly biography of Elizabeth. Has a wealth of details about the chief events that marked her reign.

Rachel and Allen Percival, *The Court of Elizabeth the First*. London: Stainer and Bell, 1976. Very interesting treatment of life in the court of Queen Elizabeth I, especially the inclusion of poetry and music.

Alison Plowden, *Marriage with My Kingdom: The Courtships of Queen Elizabeth I*. London: Book Club Associates, 1977. Lively account of the hopes and schemes of the various earls, kings, princes, and dukes who tried to become the husband of Elizabeth I.

Roger Pringle, ed., *A Portrait of Elizabeth I*. Totowa, NJ: Barnes and Noble Books, 1980. Various aspects of Elizabeth's life and reign are examined through the eyes of her contemporaries through the use of excerpts from historical documents and literary works.

A.L. Rowse, *The Elizabethan Renaissance: The Cultural Achievement*. New York: Charles Scribner's Sons, 1972. Fourth in the author's series on the England of Elizabeth; this one deals with art, literature, science, and philosophy.

———, *The Elizabethan Renaissance: The Life of the Society*. New York: Charles Scribner's Sons, 1971. Third of Rowse's four volumes on the Elizabethan era; this one deals principally with social life, including the court, social classes, and leisure activities.

Alfred L. Rowse and George B. Harrison, *Queen Elizabeth and Her Subjects*. Freeport, NY: Books for Libraries Press, 1935. Good examination of the reign of Elizabeth I, especially in its assessment of the spirit and accomplishments of the time and how it paved the way for future greatness.

Edith Sitwell, *The Queens and the Hive*. Boston: Little, Brown, 1962. This well-known poet is equally impressive in this lengthy, yet highly readable account of the life and reigns of Mary I and Elizabeth I of England and Mary, Queen of Scots.

Lacey Baldwin Smith, *The Horizon Book of the Elizabethan World*. New York: American Heritage, 1967. A comprehensive look, not only at Elizabethan England, but also at the rest of Europe and the world beyond. Also contains sections of contemporary works and quotations illustrating various aspects of the society.

Anne Somerset, *Ladies-in-Waiting: From the Tudors to the Present Day*. New York: Alfred A. Knopf, 1984. Traces developments in the roles and functions of the women who have attended the queens of England for more than five hundred years.

John Southworth, *Fools and Jesters at the English Court*. Thrupp, England: Sutton, 1998. Fascinating account of the history of the court jesters throughout English history.

David Starkey et al. *The English Court: from the Wars of the Roses to the Civil War*. London: Longman, 1987. Authors examine the various roles and functions of the court, including public image, governance, and the organization of the household.

Susan Watkins, *In Public and Private: Elizabeth I and Her World*. New York: Thames and Hudson, 1998. Entertaining and well-illustrated biography of Elizabeth I that includes not only the momentous political and religious events of the time, but also the inner workings of the queen's household.

Neville Williams, *The Life and Times of Elizabeth I*. Garden City, NY: Doubleday, 1972. Highly readable biography that examines the ways of life of all classes of people in Elizabethan England.

Violet Wilson, *Queen Elizabeth's Maids of Honour*. London: John Lane, 1922. The author's quaint style makes this account of the lives, loves, and troubles of Elizabeth's Maids of Honor all the more enjoyable.

Index

Picture Credits

About the Author

William W. Lace is a native of Fort Worth, Texas. He holds a bachelor's degree from Texas Christian University, a master's from East Texas State University, and a doctorate from the University of North Texas. After working for newspapers in Baytown, Texas, and Fort Worth, he joined the University of Texas at Arlington as sports information director and later became the director of the news service. He is now executive assistant to the chancellor for the Tarrant County College District in Fort Worth. He and his wife, Laura, live in Arlington and have two children. Lace has written numerous other works for Lucent Books, one of which—The Death Camps in the Holocaust Library series—was selected by the New York Public Library for its 1999 Recommended Teenage Reading List.